Advanced Macromedia Flash Training Course: "ActionScript in Action"

DAN LIVINGSTON

© 2002 Prentice Hall PTR

PH
PTR

Prentice Hall PTR
Upper Saddle River, New Jersey 07458

Contents

LECTURE 1   Introduction to ActionScript   1

LECTURE 2   Your First ActionScripts   19

LECTURE 3   Adding Power to ActionScripts   62

LECTURE 4   Serious Interactivity   106

LECTURE 5   Flash and XML   117

LECTURE 6   Troubleshooting ActionScript   137

LECTURE 7   Complex Scripting   155

LECTURE 8   Further Applications for Flash   186

Lecture 1

Introduction to ActionScript

Objectives

- Explain ActionScript and Object-Oriented Scripting

- Build Object and Frame Actions

- Explore and Discuss the Fundamentals of Dot Syntax, Properties, Methods, and Functions

Lesson 1.1

Explain ActionScript and Object-Oriented Scripting

What Is ActionScript?

- ActionScript is a scripting language used to control movies and objects in Flash.
  - If you want to do anything interactive in Flash, you'll need to use ActionScript.
- ActionScript looks a lot like JavaScript.
  - Macromedia did this on purpose.
- ActionScript is based on ECMA-262.
  - JavaScript is also based on ECMA-262. ActionScript in Flash 5 is based on the ECMA-262 specification, so if you've used JavaScript before, ActionScript will look familiar to you. If not, don't worry.

Notes:

_____

_____

_____

_____

_____

_____

_____

_____

What Is ActionScript Good For?

- Create multiplayer games
  - Flash games can do just about anything you want them to.
- Create engaging, user-aware navigation
  - Way beyond the world of clunky HTML and simple rollovers.
- Send data to middleware like PHP and ColdFusion
  - This allows you to interact with a database.
- Create and parse XML objects
  - ActionScript's ability to work with XML is exciting, if not full-featured.
- Communicate with JavaScript or ActiveX objects
  - This lets your Flash movie interact with the Web page it's embedded in.
- And about a billion other things.

Notes:

_____

_____

_____

_____

_____

_____

_____

_____

What ActionScript Can't Do

- ActionScript can't talk directly to a database.
  - You'll still need to use middleware like PHP, ColdFusion, or ASP to do that.
- Unicode isn't supported, but ISO-8859 and Shift-JIS are.
  - That is, both Latin and Japanese characters.
- You can't use exception handling with `try`, `throw`, or `catch`.
  - This means you can't tell your Flash movie what to do when an error occurs.

Notes:

_____

_____

_____

_____

_____

_____

_____

_____

_____

_____

Variables

Some Examples:

```
// "x" is the variable
x = 3;


// "message" is a variable that holds a string,
// i.e., usually text
message = "Please press the next button."
```

Objects and Classes

- A "class" is like a recipe.
  - If we have a "bicycle" class called "bicycle", it's a set of instructions to create a bicycle.
- An "object" is an instance of a class.
  - In this case, it would be a real bicycle, like a mountain bike or a tricycle.
- Objects have "properties."
  - In this case, properties might be height, tire size, and number of gears.
- Objects also have "methods."
  - These might be pedaling, steering, and breaking

Notes:

_____

_____

_____

_____

_____

_____

_____

_____

_____

_____

.Flash 5's Predefined Objects

- Array
- Boolean
- Color
- Date
- Key
- Math
- Mouse
- Number
- Object
- Selection
- Sound
- String
- XML
- XMLSocket

Notes:

_____

_____

_____

_____

_____

_____

_____

_____

_____

_____

Creating a Class (Advanced)

```
function HairBand(p,s)
{
        this.hair = "big";
        this.hair_dye = true;
        this.number_members = p;
        this.number_synthesizers = s;
}

function Breakup()
{
        this.hair_dye = false;
        this.hair = "crew cut";
}

// Now, actually create two objects using
// the HairBand constructor function.
kajagoogoo = new HairBand(3,4);
softcell = new HairBand(2,1500);

// Create a method for a hairband
HairBand.kajagoogoo.partyover = Breakup
```

Lesson 1.2

Building Object and Frame Actions

Basic Action Structure

```
whenSomethingHappens(input variables)
{
        do stuff
}
```

Object Actions—Movie Clips

- Object actions are chunks of ActionScript code that are attached to an object.
- Mostly, an object is a symbol that's either a button or a movie clip.
- Graphic symbols cannot have actions, nor can shapes you draw that aren't symbols.
- An object action is associated with an instance of a symbol, not with the symbol itself.
- The Object Actions panel looks like this (showing the code associated with the fish in fish_drag.fla):

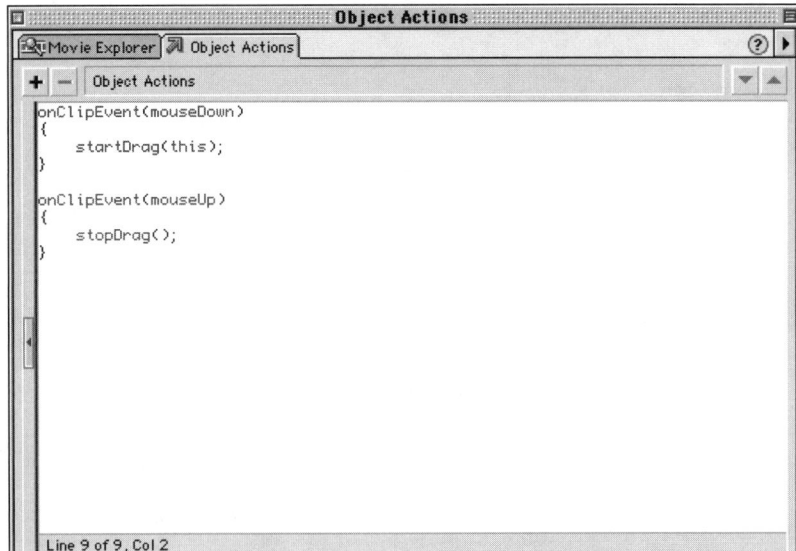

```
Object Actions
Movie Explorer | Object Actions                              ? ▶
+ − | Object Actions                                       ▼ ▲
onClipEvent(mouseDown)
{
    startDrag(this);
}

onClipEvent(mouseUp)
{
    stopDrag();
}




Line 9 of 9, Col 2
```

onClipEvents

The two functions associated with the fish in fish_drag.fla are
onClipEvents:

```
onClipEvent(mouseDown)
{
        startDrag(this);
}


onClipEvent(mouseUp)
{
        stopDrag();
}
```

This is equivalent to this:

```
onClipEvent(mouseDown)
{
        // "drag_fish" is the name of the symbol
        startDrag(_root.drag_fish);
}


onClipEvent(mouseUp)
{
        stopDrag();
}
```

- All movie clip object actions live inside an onClipEvent.
- onClipEvent is known as an event handler.
- An event is something that happens, such as the moving finishes
  loading, the user presses a mouse button, or the user hits the
  space bar. An event handler is a piece of Flash that is constantly
  looking for these events and lets ActionScript know when one of
  them occurs.
- startDrag is a method that requires a target ("this" or
  "_root.drag_fish")

Events for `onClipEvent`

- load
- unload
- enterFrame
- mouseMove
- mouseDown
- mouseUp
- keyDown
- keyUp
- data

Notes:

_____

_____

_____

_____

_____

_____

_____

_____

_____

Object Actions—Buttons

- The event handler for buttons is on instead of onClipEvent.
- The events for on are:
  - press
  - release
  - releaseOutside
  - rollOver
  - rollOut
  - dragOver
  - dragOut
  - keyPress

Notes:

_____

_____

_____

_____

_____

_____

_____

_____

_____

_____

Frame Actions

- Frame actions are like object actions, except that the actions are associated with a certain spot in the timeline instead of on an object.
- If a frame has some actions associated with it, those actions are carried out when the playhead enters that frame.
- A simple example is stopping a movie at the last frame so it doesn't loop.

Notes:

_____

_____

_____

_____

_____

_____

_____

_____

_____

_____

_____

Lesson 1.3

Explore and Discuss the Fundamentals of Dot Syntax, Properties, Methods, and Functions

Dot Syntax

If you have a movie clip called *red_shirt* inside a clip called *santa_claus*, one way to access that object is:

```
_root.santa_claus.red_shirt
```

`_root` is the base of all Flash movies. If you want to find out where *red_shirt* is on the Stage, you could use:

```
xPosition = _root.santa_claus.red_shirt._x;
```

Dot Syntax (from JavaScript)

```
document.myForm.textBox.value = "Try again!";
```

or

```
document.image['nav'].src = 'images/clickme.gif';
```

Properties

Some examples of movie clip properties are:

- How wide it is (_width)
- Where it is on the Stage (_x and _y)
- What frame is currently being played (_currentframe)
- How transparent it is (_alpha)
- Its name (_name)
- Whether it's visible or not (_visible)

Properties can be read or altered:

```
// read
clueWidth = _root.clue._width;

// altered
_root.clue._width = 110;
```

or

```
_root.clue._width = _root.clue._width - 40;
```

Notes:

_____

_____

_____

_____

_____

_____

Methods

Some examples of what methods can do are:

- Stop a movie clip
- Go to a certain frame and start playing there
- See if a movie clip is over another movie clip
- Hide the mouse cursor
- Calculate a cosine
- Set the volume of a sound being played

Method Example

To start a movie playing at frame 10:

```
clue.gotoAndPlay(10);
```

The method here is gotoAndPlay. All methods live inside objects—they don't exist on their own.

Notes:

_____

_____

_____

_____

_____

_____

Functions

- You can create your own objects, properties, and methods using constructor functions.
- A function is a set of instructions that's executed only a certain times.
- Functions can look and act a lot like methods.

Notes:

_____

_____

_____

_____

_____

_____

_____

_____

_____

_____

_____

Lecture 2

Your First
ActionScripts

Objectives

- Explore the Actions Panels

- Move from Scene to Scene Using Buttons and Event Handlers

- Handle Events with Movie Clips

- Change Movie Clip Properties

- Create a Movie Using Text Fields, Arrays, and Loops

Lesson 2.1

Explore the Actions Panels

The Panels

The same panel serves for both frame actions and object actions.

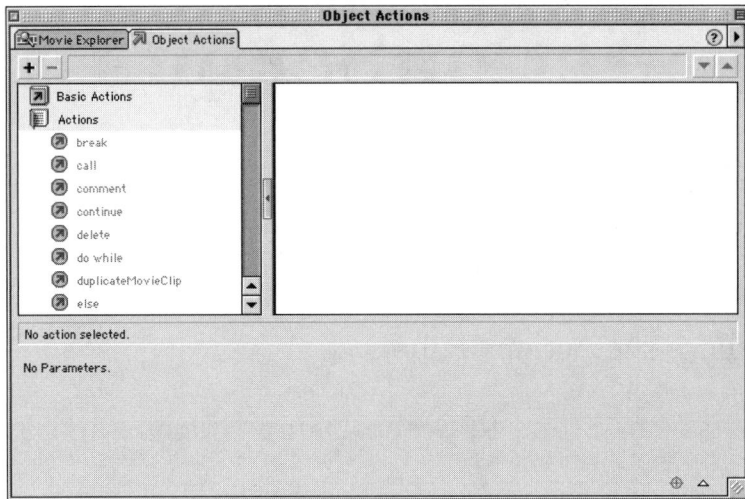

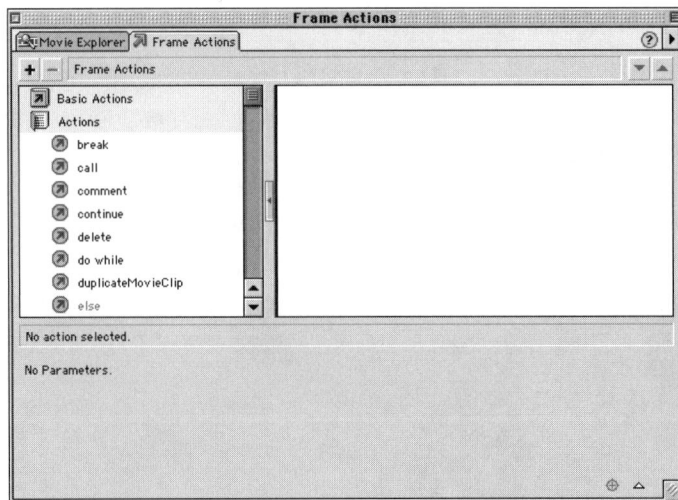

Parts of an Actions Panel

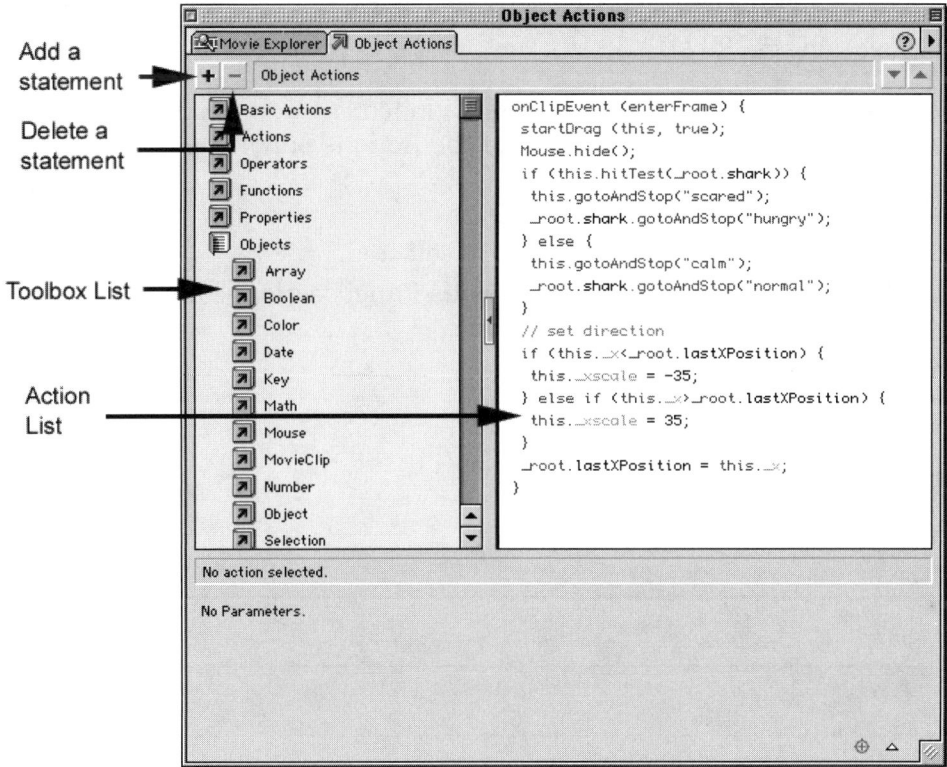

Add a
statement

Delete a
statement

Toolbox List

Action
List

```
Object Actions

Movie Explorer   Object Actions                                    ?  ▶

+  -   Object Actions                                              ▼  ▲

Basic Actions          onClipEvent (enterFrame) {
Actions                 startDrag (this, true);
Operators               Mouse.hide();
Functions               if (this.hitTest(_root.shark)) {
Properties               this.gotoAndStop("scared");
Objects                  _root.shark.gotoAndStop("hungry");
   Array               } else {
   Boolean               this.gotoAndStop("calm");
   Color                 _root.shark.gotoAndStop("normal");
   Date                 }
   Key                  // set direction
   Math                 if (this._x<_root.lastXPosition) {
   Mouse                 this._xscale = -35;
   MovieClip            } else if (this._x>_root.lastXPosition) {
   Number                this._xscale = 35;
   Object               }
   Selection            _root.lastXPosition = this._x;
                        }

No action selected.

No Parameters.
```

Normal Mode Versus Expert Mode

- Normal = The program helps you code
- Expert = You type in the code yourself

Using Expert mode is strongly recommended.
To make Expert mode the default of the Actions panels:

1. Choose Edit → Preferences.
2. Make sure the General tab is selected.
3. Near the bottom, in the Actions Panel section, change mode from Normal Mode to Expert Mode.
4. Click OK.

Notes:

_____

_____

_____

_____

_____

_____

_____

_____

_____

_____

Lesson 2.2

Move from Scene to Scene Using Buttons and Event Handlers

Code in This Lesson

- `stop()`
  - Stops the current movie
- `on(release, keyPress)`
  - Tells movie to watch for the user releasing the mouse button or pressing a key on the keyboard
- `gotoAndPlay()`
  - Goes to a certain place in a movie and starts playing at that frame

Notes:

_____

_____

_____

_____

_____

_____

_____

_____

_____

buzzkill1.fla

Move Beyond the First Scene

1. Open the file `buzzkill1.fla`, which you copied to your hard drive at the beginning of this lecture.
2. Notice that there are three scenes—one for each slide. Each scene has one frame action on its last frame:
   ```
   stop().
   ```
3. Click on the last frame in the actions layer in each scene, and then choose Window → Actions to see the Action-Script. The only ActionScript you'll see is `stop()`.This stop method halts the playhead in its tracks; that is, it stops the Flash movie from playing further.
4. Go ahead and play with movie, using Control → Test Movie . Always test your movies with Control → Test Movie, because that's the only way you can properly test your actions.
5. Notice that there's no way to go beyond the first scene/ slide.
6. Close the window with the movie playing.
7. Go to the last frame in Scene 1 of the movie (frame 60) on the button layer.
8. Insert → Keyframe.
9. Window → Library.
10. Drag the Forward Button symbol onto the empty button layer. Make sure you're still on frame 60. Position the button wherever you want.
11. Click on the button.
12. Window → Actions.
13. Enter this code:
    ```
    on(release)
    {
       gotoAndPlay("Scene 2","slide2");
    }
    ```
14. Control → Test Movie. Once the movie is playing, pressing the button should send you to the next scene.

buzzkill1.fla

Add Two Buttons on the Second Scene

1. Open up Scene 2.
2. Open up the Library if it isn't already open.
3. Go to the last frame in the movie (40) on the empty button layer.
4. Insert →Keyframe.
5. Drag the Backward Button and the Forward Button to the Stage and place them wherever you like.
6. Click on the Forward Button.
7. Open up the Actions panel if it isn't open.
8. Enter this code:
   ```
   on(release)
   {
     gotoAndPlay("Scene 3","slide3");
   }
   ```
9. Click on the Backward Button.
10. Enter this code:
    ```
    on(release)
    {
      gotoAndPlay("Scene 1","slide1");
    }
    ```
11. Save the file and Control →Test Movie.

buzzkill1.fla

Add the Last Button to the Final Scene

1. Open up Scene 3.
2. Open up the Library (Window →Library) if it isn't already open.
3. Go to the last frame in Scene 3 on the button layer (frame 45).
4. Drag the Backward Button to the Stage and place it wherever you like.
5. Click on the Backward Button.
6. Open up the Actions panel if it isn't open.
7. Enter this code:
   ```
   on(release)
   {
      gotoAndPlay("Scene 2","slide2");
   }
   ```
8. Control →Test Movie!

buzzkill1.fla

Move Forward Using the Space Bar or the Right Arrow

1. Go back to the Forward Button on frame 60 of Scene 1.
2. Click on the button and open its Actions panel.
3. Add this code:

```
on(release, keyPress "<space>")
{
  gotoAndPlay("Scene 2", "slide2");
}
on(keyPress "<right>")
{
  gotoAndPlay("Scene 2", "slide2");
}
```

4. Control →Test Movie.

Scene 2 Backward Button

```
// This button only needs one function, since only
// one key can be used to go backwards, as opposed to
// two keys to go forward.
on(release, keyPress "<left>")
{
  gotoAndPlay("Scene 1", "slide1");
}
```

Scene 2 Forward Button

```
on(release, keyPress "<space>")
{
  gotoAndPlay("Scene 3", "slide3");
}
on(keyPress "<right>")
{
  gotoAndPlay("Scene 3", "slide3");
}
```

Scene 3 Backward Button

```
on(release, keyPress "<left>")
{
  gotoAndPlay("Scene 2", "slide2");
}
```

Events the on Event Handler Can Recognize

- press
- release
- releaseOutside
- rollOver
- rollOut
- dragOver
- dragOut
- keyPress

Notes:

_____

_____

_____

_____

_____

_____

_____

_____

_____

_____

Lesson 2.3

Handle Events with Movie Clips

Code in this Lesson

- onClipEvent()
- trace()
- startDrag
- if()
- hitTest()
- this
- gotoAndStop()

Notes:

_____

_____

_____

_____

_____

_____

_____

_____

drag_jake1.fla

trace

1. Open `drag_jake1.fla`.
2. Click on Jake the Fish (as opposed to the pea shark).
3. Open the Actions panel (it should say "Object Actions" at the top).
4. Enter this code:
   ```
   onClipEvent(enterFrame)
   {
      trace("mouse in movie");
   }
   ```
5. Control →Test Movie.

onClipEvent()

1. Click on Jake.
2. Open the Actions panel.
3. Change the code to:
   ```
   onClipEvent(enterFrame)
   {
      startDrag(this, true);
   }
   ```
4. Control →Test Movie.

if and hitTest

Conditional Logic (`if`)

```
if(condition)
{
    statements;
}
```

drag_jake1.fla

Conditional Logic (if)

1. Get to Jake's Actions panel.
2. Enter this code:

```
onClipEvent(enterFrame)
{
  startDrag(this, true);
  if(this.hitTest(_root.shark))
  {
        this.gotoAndStop("scared");
  }
}
```

3. Control →Test Movie

Examples of Conditions

All conditions evaluate to "true" or "false":

- `x == 5`
- `_root._xmouse < 94`
- `this.hitTest(_root.shark)`

Notes:

hitTest

```
movieClip1.hitTest(movieClip2)
this.hitTest(shark)
// To start looking at the top of the movie, use "_root"
this.hitTest(_root.shark);

// Finally:
this.gotoAndStop("scared");
```

drag_jake1.fla

Finish the movie by entering this code into Jake's Actions panel:

```
onClipEvent(enterFrame)
{
  startDrag(this, true);
  if(this.hitTest(_root.shark))
  {
        this.gotoAndStop("scared");
        _root.shark.gotoAndStop("hungry");
  }
  else
  {
        this.gotoAndStop("calm");
        _root.shark.gotoAndStop("normal");
  }
}
```

Lesson 2.4

Change Movie Clip Properties

Movie Clip Properties Code

- `onClipEvent(keyDown)`
- `Key.getCode()`
- `Key.LEFT, Key.RIGHT, Key.UP, Key.DOWN`
- `_x, _y, _xmouse, _ymouse`
- `_alpha, _rotation`
- `_xscale, _yscale`
- `getBounds()`
- `startDrag()`
- `stopDrag()`

Notes:

_____

_____

_____

_____

_____

_____

_____

drag_props1.fla

Move the Fish with the Left Arrow Key Using
onClipEvent(keyDown)

1. Open `drag_props1.fla`.
2. Click on the fish.
3. Open the Actions panel (make sure it's Object Actions).
4. Enter this code:

```
//keyDown acts like keyPress
onClipEvent(keyDown)
{
   if(Key.getCode() == Key.LEFT)
   {
        this._x = this._x - 3;
   }
}
```

5. Control →Test Movie. You can move the fish to the left by pressing the left arrow key. It works if you hold the key down as well.

if (Key.getCode() == Key.LEFT)

```
onClipEvent(keyDown)
{
  // "Key" is a new object that knows
  // which key was pressed
  if(Key.getCode() == Key.LEFT)
  {
        this._x = this._x - 3;
  }
}
```

Key.getCode()

```
// One of the methods associated
// with the Key object is getCode().
// The getCode() method returns the
// character code of the last key
// pressed.

if(Key.getCode() == Key.LEFT)
```

Key.KEYNAME

Key.KEYNAME is a shortcut to a key's character code. It's much more convenient than remembering the actual character code.

```
if(Key.getCode() == Key.LEFT)
```

is the same as:

```
if(Key.getCode() == 37)
```

_x

```
onClipEvent(keyDown)
{
  if(Key.getCode() == Key.LEFT)
  {
        // _x is horizontal position
        this._x = this._x - 3;
  }
}
```

_x is the movie clip's horizontal position, measured from the left edge of the movie to the movie clip's center.

```
// move the movie clip 3 pixels
// to the left
this._x = this._x - 3;
```

if, elseif & else

```
if(condition1) { code }
else if(condition2) { code }
else { code }
```

Instead of:

```
if(condition1) { code }
if(cond.2 is true and cond.1 is false)
  { code }
if(cond.1 and cond.2 are false) { code }
```

drag_props1.fla

Add the Rest of the Arrows—The Whole Code

```
onClipEvent(keyDown)
{
  if(Key.getCode() == Key.LEFT)
  {
       this._x = this._x - 3;
  }
  else if(Key.getCode() == Key.RIGHT)
  {
       this._x = this._x + 3;
  }
  else if(Key.getCode() == Key.UP)
  {
       this._y = this._y - 3;
  }
  else if(Key.getCode() == Key.DOWN)
  {
       this._y = this._y + 3;
  }
}
```

`_alpha`

- The alpha property controls the opacity of a movie clip
- An alpha setting of 100 means the movie clip is completely opaque.
- An alpha setting of 0 means the movie clip is completely transparent; that is, invisible.

Notes:

_____

_____

_____

_____

_____

_____

_____

_____

_____

_____

_____

_____

_____

drag_props2.fla

Add a Slider

1. Open drag_props2.fla.
2. Notice there are some new pieces on the stage: some extra text, a slider bar, and a slider. Also, notice that each instance has a different name. This is a necessary thing—otherwise, Flash doesn't know which instance is what.
3. Go to the first frame of the actions layer, and go to Window →Actions. Make sure you're entering a frame action.
4. Enter this code:

```
// Get boundaries and position of the slider bar
alphaBounds = alphaBar.getBounds(_root);
_root.alphaBarXMin = alphaBounds.xMin;
_root.alphaBarXMax = alphaBounds.xMax;
_root.alphaBarYMid = alphaBar._y;
// Set slider position on slider bar
alphaSlider._x = _root.alphaBarXMin;
alphaSlider._y =_root.alphaBarYMid;
```

alphaBounds Object

The getBounds method returns an object with four properties. In this case, we called the object alphaBounds.

The alphaBounds object has four properties:

```
alphaBounds.xMin
alphaBounds.xMax
alphaBounds.yMin
alphaBounds.yMax
```

Global Variables

```
// Get boundaries and position of slider bar
alphaBounds = alphaBar.getBounds(_root);

// Create global variables
_root.alphaBarXMin = alphaBounds.xMin;
_root.alphaBarXMax = alphaBounds.xMax;
_root.alphaBarYMid = alphaBar._y;
```

Local Variables

Local variables only exist within a set of curly braces.

```
onClipEvent(enterFrame)
{ x = 5; }

onClipEvent(keyDown)
{
  // The variable "x" isn't recognized
  trace(x);
}
```

Local to Global Variables

```
onClipEvent(enterFrame)
{
  _root.x = 5;
}

onClipEvent(keyDown)
{
  // The variable "x" is now recognized
  trace(_root.x);
}
```

Positioning the Slider

```
// Get boundaries and position of slider bar
alphaBounds = alphaBar.getBounds(_root);
_root.alphaBarXMin = alphaBounds.xMin;
_root.alphaBarXMax = alphaBounds.xMax;
_root.alphaBarYMid = alphaBar._y;

// Set slider position on slider bar
alphaSlider._x = _root.alphaBarXMin;
alphaSlider._y = _root.alphaBarYMid;
```

Making the Slider Slide

- The slider only slides along the slider bar.
- The slider moves only if the user presses down the mouse button while on top of the slider.
- When the user releases the mouse button, the slider stops moving.

Expanding `startDrag ()`

Here's the syntax:

```
startDrag(movieClipName, true/false, leftEdge, topEdge,
rightEdge, bottomEdge)
```

All those edges define a box that limits where the object can be dragged. Edges are defined by pixels.

Stopping the Slider

Stopping the slider is simple:

```
onClipEvent(mouseUp)
{
   stopDrag();
}
```

You don't need to specify which object is stopped, because only one movie clip can be dragged at one time.

Multiple Conditions

Suppose you have two conditions, A and B. If both of them must be true, here's the code you would use:

```
if (A && B)
{ blah; }
```

&& stands for "and"

drag_props2.fla

Finish the `_alpha` Slider

1. Because we're thorough little coders, we create the variable in the frame action of the actions layer. Add this line to the existing variables:

   ```
   _root.alphaDrag = false;
   ```

2. Now, go back to the slider's actions, and make the code look like this:

   ```
   onClipEvent(mouseDown)
   {
   // Get the boundaries for the slider
   bounds = this.getBounds(_root);
   // See if the user clicked inside the slider
   if((_root._xmouse <= bounds.xMax) &&
   (_root._xmouse >= bounds.xMin) &&
   (_root._ymouse <= bounds.yMax) &&
   (_root._ymouse >= bounds.yMin))
   {
   startDrag(this, true, _root.alphaBarXMin,
   _root.alphaBarYMid, _root.alphaBarXMax,
   _root.alphaBarYMid);
   _root.alphaDrag = true;
   }
   }
   onClipEvent(mouseUp) {
   stopDrag ();
   _root.alphaDrag = false;
   }
   onClipEvent(enterFrame)
   {
   if(_root.alphaDrag)
   {
   xPos = _root._xmouse;
   percentage = 100 * ((_root.alphaBarXMax -
   xPos)/(_root.alphaBarXMax - _root.alphaBarXMin));
   _root.fish._alpha = percentage;
   }
   }
   ```

drag_props3.fla

_yscale

1. Open `drag_props3.fla`.
2. Don't panic. We've done all the hard work already. To make these sliders work, and do what we want them to, it's a matter of copying, pasting, and tweaking.
3. Click on the first frame in the actions layer, and open up the Frame Actions panel.
4. Enter the following code:

```
// Set variables
alphaBounds = _root.alphaBar.getBounds(_root);
_root.alphaBarXMin = alphaBounds.xMin;
_root.alphaBarXMax = alphaBounds.xMax;
_root.alphaBarYMid = _root.alphaBar._y;
heightBounds = _root.heightBar.getBounds(_root);
_root.heightBarXMin = heightBounds.xMin;
_root.heightBarXMax = heightBounds.xMax;
_root.heightBarYMid = _root.heightBar._y;
widthBounds = _root.widthBar.getBounds(_root);
_root.widthBarXMin = widthBounds.xMin;
_root.widthBarXMax = widthBounds.xMax;
_root.widthBarYMid = _root.widthBar._y;
rotateBounds = _root.rotateBar.getBounds(_root);
_root.rotateBarXMin = rotateBounds.xMin;
_root.rotateBarXMax = rotateBounds.xMax;
_root.rotateBarYMid = _root.rotateBar._y;
_root.alphaDrag = false;
_root.heightDrag = false;
_root.widthDrag = false;
_root.rotateDrag = false;
// set slider positions
_root.alphaSlider._x = _root.alphaBarXMin;
_root.alphaSlider._y =_root.alphaBarYMid;
_root.heightSlider._x = (_root.heightBarXMin +
_root.heightBarXMax)/2;
_root.heightSlider._y =_root.heightBarYMid;
_root.widthSlider._x = (_root.widthBarXMin +
_root.widthBarXMax)/2;
_root.widthSlider._y =_root.widthBarYMid;
_root.rotateSlider._x = (_root.rotateBarXMin +
```

```
_root.rotateBarXMax)/2;
_root.rotateSlider._y =_root.rotateBarYMid;
```

5. Remember, don't panic. All we're doing is copying the code from the alpha code and pasting it four times. Then, we're tweaking it some so that we have four separately named sliders and slider bars. There's only one small difference—the latest sliders are positioned in the middle of the bar instead of on the end.

6. Click on the slider under the _yscale heading. The slider's name is heightSlider.

7. Enter the following code (it should look familiar):

```
onClipEvent (mouseDown)
{
// get the boundaries for the slider
bounds = this.getBounds(_root);
if((_root._xmouse <= bounds.xMax) &&
(_root._xmouse >= bounds.xMin) &&
(_root._ymouse <= bounds.yMax) &&
(_root._ymouse >= bounds.yMin))
{
startDrag(this, true, _root.heightBarXMin,
_root.heightBarYMid, _root.heightBarXMax,
_root.heightBarYMid);
_root.heightDrag = true;
}
}
onClipEvent (mouseUp) {
stopDrag();
_root.heightDrag = false;
}
onClipEvent (enterFrame)
{
if(_root.heightDrag)
{
xPos = _root._xmouse;
percentage = 200 * (( xPos -_
root.heightBarXMin)/(_root.heightBarXMax -
_root.heightBarXMin));
//trace(percentage);
_root.fish._yscale = percentage;
}
}
```

8. Control →Test Movie .

drag_props3.fla

_xscale

1. Click on the `xscale` slider. It's called `widthSlider`.
2. Open the Object Actions panel.
3. Enter the following code:

```
onClipEvent(mouseDown)
{
// Get the boundaries for the slider
bounds = this.getBounds(_root);
// see if the user clicked inside the slider
if((_root._xmouse <= bounds.xMax) &&
(_root._xmouse >= bounds.xMin) &&
(_root._ymouse <= bounds.yMax) &&
(_root._ymouse >= bounds.yMin))
{
startDrag(this, true, _root.widthBarXMin,
_root.widthBarYMid, _root.widthBarXMax,
_root.widthBarYMid);
_root.widthDrag = true;
}
}
onClipEvent(mouseUp) {
stopDrag();
_root.widthDrag = false;
}
onClipEvent(enterFrame)
{
if(_root.widthDrag)
{
xPos = _root._xmouse;
percentage = 200 * (( xPos -_
root.widthBarXMin)/(_root.widthBarXMax -_
root.widthBarXMin));
_root.fish._xscale = percentage;
}
}
```

4. Test the movie.

drag_props3.fla

_rotation

1. Click on the slider under the _rotation heading.
2. Open up the Object Actions panel.
3. Enter this code:

```
onClipEvent(mouseDown)
{
// Get the boundaries for the slider
bounds = this.getBounds(_root);
// see if the user clicked inside the slider
if((_root._xmouse <= bounds.xMax) &&
(_root._xmouse >= bounds.xMin) &&
(_root._ymouse <= bounds.yMax) &&
(_root._ymouse >= bounds.yMin))
{
//trace("rotate on");
startDrag(this, true, _root.rotateBarXMin,
_root.rotateBarYMid, _root.rotateBarXMax,
_root.rotateBarYMid);
_root.rotateDrag = true;
}
}
onClipEvent(mouseUp) {
stopDrag ();
_root.rotateDrag = false;
}
onClipEvent(enterFrame)
{
if(_root.rotateDrag)
{
xPos = _root._xmouse;
percentage = ( xPos -_
root.rotateBarXMin)/(_root.rotateBarXMax -
_root.rotateBarXMin);
rotation = (percentage * 720) - 360
_root.fish._rotation = rotation;
}
}
```

4. Test that movie.

Lesson 2.5

Create a Movie Using Text Fields, Arrays, and Loops

Text Fields

Three kinds of text fields:

- static: you've already used this kind
- dynamic: text associated with a variable that can be changed via ActionScript
- input: just like dynamic text, but the user can enter in their own text.

"Make Irving's Face" uses all three kinds

Notes:

_____

_____

_____

_____

_____

_____

_____

_____

Arrays

Here's an example:

```
arrayName[0] = 5
arrayName[1] = "hi there"
arrayName[2] = true
arrayName[3] = "this is the fourth element in this array"
```

or:

```
myFriends[0] = "Tanya"
myFriends[1] = "Jonathan"
myFriends[2] = "Sarah Jane"
myFriends[3] = "Mark & Spencer"
```

Note that the first element in all arrays is element number zero, not one.

Looping

Syntax:

```
for(initial condition; end condition; counter increment)
{
statements;
}
```

For example:

```
for(loopCounter = 1, loopCounter < 10, loopCounter++)
{
trace(loopCounter);
}
```

This would result in the numbers 0 through 9 listed in the Output window.

`do_while` Loops

Syntax:

```
do {
statements;
} while(condition)
```

For Example:

```
loopCounter = 1;
do {
trace(loopCounter);
loopCounter = loopCounter + 1;
} while(loopCounter < 10)
```

irving1.fla

Creating the Irving Movie

The Irv symbol has five frames. Each frame is labeled. They are:

- sad
- mad
- happy
- scared
- blank

1. Open the file `irving1.fla`.
2. Click on the first frame of the actions layer.
3. Open the Frame Actions panel.
4. Enter the following code:
   ```
   // Create face array
   faceArray = new
   Array("happy","sad","mad","scared","blank")
   ```
5. Click on the Do it! button.
6. Open the Object Actions panel.
7. Enter the following code:
   ```
   on(release)
   {
   // loop through array and see
   // if irvMood matches anything in the
   // faceArray. If so, go to that label in the Irv
   for(i=0; i<5; i++)
   {
   if(_root.irvMood == faceArray[i])
   {
   _root.irv.gotoAndStop(faceArray[i]);
   break;
   }
   }
   _root.lastIrvMood = _root.irvMood;
   }
   ```
4. Control →Test Movie. Type in one of the five possible moods and click the Do it! button to see Irving's face change.

Associative Arrays

An element in an array can be identified by a string as well as a number.

```
assocArray = new Array();
assocArray["happy"] = "ice cream";
assocArray["sad"] = "George W. Bush";
assocArray["excited"] = "You found gold!";
```

Summary

Here's a list of everything we covered in this lecture:

```
_x                                    if
_y                                    elseif
_xmouse                               else
_ymouse                               Text fields
_alpha                                Looping (for, break)
Arrays

Global variables                      Key.getCode
startDrag                             Key.KEYNAME
hitTest                              onClipEvent(enter
                                      Frame, keyDown,
getBounds                             mouseUp, mouseDown)
gotoAndPlay
gotoAndStop                           on(release, key Press)
trace
```

Lecture 3

Adding Power to ActionScripts

Objectives

- Create a Simple Space Game Using Skills from Lecture 2

- Power Handle Movie Clips with `duplicateMovieClip`, `removeMovieClip`, `loadMovie`, `unloadMovie`, **and** `attachMovie`

- Explore the Movie Explorer

Lesson 3.1

Create a Simple Space Game Using Skills from Lecture 2

Code In This Lecture

- `_visible`
- `duplicateMovieClip`
- `removeMovieClip`
- `loadMovie`
- `unloadMovie`
- `_rotate`
- `getProperty`
- `attachMovie`
- `Math`
- `setProperty`

Notes:

_____

_____

_____

_____

_____

_____

_____

_____

_____

_____

space_game.fla

Text Files with Actions

The files containing the code from this lesson are named as follows:

- Frame Action   =   `list3-1.txt`
- Hero Rocket Ship   =   `list3-2.txt`
- Yellow Pellet Shot   =   `list3-3.txt`
- Manta Ship   =   `list3-4.txt`
- Manta Ship Shot   =   `list3-5.txt`
- Spike Ship   =   `list3-6.txt`
- Spike Ship Shot   =   `list3-7.txt`

Notes:

_____

_____

_____

_____

_____

_____

_____

_____

_____

_____

space_game.fla

The Frame Action

```
//set variables
ourHeroShotInAir = false;
ourHeroDead = false;

// set enemy ship variables
mantaDead = false;
mantaShotInAir = false;
spikeDead = true;
spikeShotInAir = false;
enemyDirection = "right";
lastEnemyAlive = "spike";

// set properties
shot._visible = false;
mantaShot._visible = false;
spikeShot._visible = false;
spike._visible = false;
```

space_game.fla

The Our Hero Rocket Ship

```
onClipEvent(enterFrame)
{
        startDrag( this, true, 50, 300, 500, 375 );

        // see if ourHero got nailed
        if(this.hitTest(_root.mantaShot) &&
          !_root.ourHeroDead)
        {
                _root.ourHeroDead = true;
                this.gotoAndPlay("pow");
        }

        // reset ourHero's ship
        if(this._currentframe == 35)
        {
                _root.ourHeroDead = false;
                this.gotoAndPlay("start");
        }
}

onClipEvent(mouseUp)
{
        if(!_root.ourHeroShotInAir)
        {
                _root.shot._x = this._x;
                _root.shot._y = this._y - 50;
                _root.shot._visible = true;
                _root.ourHeroShotInAir = true;
        }
}
```

space_game.fla

The Yellow Pellet Shot

```
onClipEvent(enterFrame)
{
        // see if ourHero's shot is in the air
        if(_root.ourHeroShotInAir)
        {
                if(this._y > 0)
                {
                        this._y = this._y - 20;
                }
                else
                {
                        _root.ourHeroShotInAir =
                          false;
                        this._visible = false;
                }
        }
}
```

space_game.fla

The Manta Ship

```
// manta ship
onClipEvent(enterFrame)
{
        // see if manta was hit
        if(this.hitTest(_root.shot) && !_root.mantaDead)
        {
                _root.shot._visible = false;
                _root.lastEnemyAlive = "manta";
                _root.mantaDead = true;
                _root.manta.gotoAndPlay("pow");
        }

        // see if the manta just finished playing
          explosion
        if(this._currentframe == 11 && _root.
          lastEnemyAlive == "manta")
        {
                // bring spike to life
                _root.spikeDead = false;
                _root.spike._visible = true;
                _root.spike.gotoAndStop("start");
        }

        // move the manta
        if(_root.enemyDirection == "right")
        {
                if(this._x < 450)
                {
                        this._x = this._x + 10;
                }
                else
                {
                        _root.enemyDirection =
                          "left";
                        this._x = this._x - 10;
                }
```

```
          }
          else
          {
                    if(this._x>100)
                    {
                              this._x = this._x - 10;
                    }
                    else
                    {
                              _root.enemyDirection =
                                "right";
                              this._x = this._x + 10;
                    }
          }
    }
```

space_game.fla

The Manta Ship Shot

```
// manta shot
onClipEvent(enterFrame)
{
        // see if it's appropriate for the manta to fire
          now
        if(!_root.mantaShotInAir && !_root.mantaDead)
        {
                this._x = _root.manta._x;
                this._y = _root.manta._y;
                this._visible = true;
                _root.mantaShotInAir = true;
        }
        else
        {
                // see if shot is off the screen
                if(this._y > 400)
                {
                        this._visible = false;
                        _root.mantaShotInAir =
                          false;
                }
                else
                {
                        this._y = this._y + 20;
                }
        }
}
```

space_game.fla

The Spike Ship

```
// spike ship
onClipEvent(enterFrame)
{
        // see if spike was hit
        if(this.hitTest(_root.shot) && !_root.spikeDead)
        {
                    _root.shot._visible = false;
                    _root.spikeDead = true;
                    _root.lastEnemyAlive = "spike";
                    _root.spike.gotoAndPlay("pow");
        }

        // see if the spike just finished playing
          explosion
        if(this._currentframe > 10 && _root.lastEnemyAlive
          == "spike")
        {
                    // bring manta to life
                    _root.mantaDead = false;
                    _root.manta._visible = true;
                    _root.manta.gotoAndStop("start");
        }

        // move the spike
        if(_root.spikeDirection == "right")
        {
                    if(this._x<450)
                    {
                                this._x = this._x+10;
                    } else {
                                _root.spikeDirection =
                                   "left";
                    }
        }
        else
        {
                    if(this._x>100)
```

```
                    {
                              this._x = this._x-10;
                    } else {
                              _root.spikeDirection =
                                "right";
                    }
          }
}
```

space_game.fla

The Spike Ship Shot

```
// spikeShot
onClipEvent(enterFrame)
{
        // see if it's appropriate for the spike to fire
          now
        if(!_root.spikeShotInAir && !_root.spikeDead)
        {
                this._x = _root.spike._x;
                this._y = _root.spike._y;
                this._visible = true;
                _root.spikeShotInAir = true;
        }
        else
        {

                // see if shot is off the screen
                if(this._y > 400)
                {
                        this._visible = false;
                        _root.spikeShotInAir =
                          false;
                }
                else
                {
                        this._y = this._y + 40;
                }
        }
}
```

Text Files with Actions

The files containing the code from this lesson are named as follows:

- Frame Action   =   `list3-1.txt`
- Hero Rocket Ship   =   `list3-2.txt`
- Yellow Pellet Shot   =   `list3-3.txt`
- Manta Ship   =   `list3-4.txt`
- Manta Ship Shot   =   `list3-5.txt`
- Spike Ship   =   `list3-6.txt`
- Spike Ship Shot   =   `list3-7.txt`

Notes:

_____

_____

_____

_____

_____

_____

_____

_____

_____

Lesson 3.2

Power Handle Movie Clips with `duplicateMovieClip`, `removeMovieClip`, `loadMovie`, `unloadMovie`, and `attachMovie`

Power Handling Movie Clips

Power handling means:

- Making copies of movie clips (`duplicateMovieClip`)
- Removing copies of movie clips (`removeMovieClip`)
- Loading whole movies from another URL into your page (`load-Movie`)
- Unloading them again (`unloadMovie`)
- Attaching movies from the Library onto your playing movie clip, even if that attached movie wasn't originally in your movie (`attachMovie`)

Notes:

_____

_____

_____

_____

_____

_____

_____

Background: Levels

- The movie that opens the Flash player is automatically placed on level 0.
- Any other SWF movies that are loaded into that Flash player can be specified to load in level 0, replacing the original movie, or can be put into any other level above the original movie (level 1, 2, 198, etc.).
- Any movie that is loaded above the level 0 movie has a transparent stage.
- Any time you load a movie on a level that is currently occupied by another movie, it is replaced by the newly loaded movie.

Notes:

_____

_____

_____

_____

_____

_____

_____

_____

_____

duplicate1.fla

Duplicate a Single Movie Clip and Place It on Another Level

1. Open the file `duplicate1.fla` that you copied to your hard drive at the start of this lecture.
2. Just a circle with a blue-to-black radial gradient. If you look in edit symbol mode at the mc_ball animation by double-clicking the instance on the stage, the size of the ball also changes, along with the placement of the gradient, over 30 frames.
3. Click on the ball and open its Object Actions panel.
4. Enter this code:

```
onClipEvent (mouseUp)
{
        this.duplicateMovieClip("ball1", 1);
        _root.ball1._x = Math.random() * 500;
        _root.ball1._y = Math.random() * 400;
}
```

5. Test the movie.

duplicate1.fla

Duplicate a Single Movie Clip Multiple Times Without _name

1. With `duplicate1.fla` still open, go to the frame in the actions layer.
2. Open the Frame Actions panel.
3. Enter this code:
   ```
   // initialize counter variable
   counter = 1;
   ```
4. Click on the ball and make sure its Object Actions panel is open.
5. Enter this code:
   ```
   onClipEvent(mouseUp)
   {
           this.duplicateMovieClip("ball" +
             _root.counter, _root.counter);
           setProperty("_root.ball" + _root.counter, _x,
             Math.random() * 500);
           setProperty("_root.ball" + _root.counter, _y,
             Math.random() * 400);
           _root.counter = _root.counter + 1;

   }
   ```
6. Test the movie.

setProperty

Example:

```
setProperty(shark, _alpha, 50);
```

has the same effect as:

```
shark._alpha = 50;
```

Why Use setProperty?

- Dynamically create movie clip names
- The name of the movie clip is:
  ```
  _root.ball Åg_root.counterÅh
  ```
- What we want to create is something like:
  ```
  _root.ball24 or _root.ball15
  ```

Notes:

_____

_____

_____

_____

_____

_____

_____

duplicate1.fla

Duplicate a Single Movie Clip Multiple Times Using `_name`

1. With `duplicate1.fla` still open, go to the frame in the actions layer.
2. Open the Frame Actions panel.
3. Enter this code:
   ```
   // initialize counter variable
   counter = 1;
   ```
4. Click on the ball and make sure its Object Actions panel is open.
5. Enter this code:
   ```
   onClipEvent(mouseUp)
   {
           if(this._name == "ball")
           {
                   this.duplicateMovieClip("ball" +
                     _root.counter, _root.counter);
                   setProperty("_root.ball" +
                     _root.counter, _x, Math.
                     random() * 500);
                   setProperty("_root.ball" +
                     _root.counter, _y, Math.
                     random() * 400);
                   _root.counter = _root.counter +
                     1;
           }
   }
   ```
6. Test the movie.

duplicate1.fla

Removing Movie Clips

1. Click on the ball and make sure the Object Actions panel is open.
2. Change the code to include this new if statement:

```
onClipEvent(mouseUp)
{
if(this._name == "ball")
        {
                        this.duplicateMovieClip("ball" +
_root.counter, _root.counter);
                        setProperty("_root.ball" +
_root.counter, _x, Math.random() * 500);
                        setProperty("_root.ball" +
_root.counter, _y, Math.random() * 400);
                        if(_root.counter > 10)
                        {
                                        removeMovieClip
                                        ("_root.ball" +
                                        (_root.counter-
                                        10));
                        }
                        _root.counter = _root.counter +
                          1;
        }
    }
```

3. Test the movie to see how this works.

spinner1.fla

Duplicating with Purpose: Example 1

1. Open the file `spinner1.fla`, which you copied to your hard drive at the start of this lecture.
2. We start with a single instance called circle on the stage.
3. By creating a single frame action:

```
counter = 1
```

4. And then adding this code to the circle object:

```
onClipEvent(enterFrame)
{
        if(this._name == "circle" && _root.counter <
          50)
        {
                this.duplicateMovieClip
                  ("circle"+ _root.counter,
                  _root.counter);
                setProperty("_root.circle"+
                  _root.counter, _rotation,
                  _root.counter*2);
                setProperty("_root.circle" +
                  _root.counter, _xscale, 100-
                  (2*_root.counter));
                setProperty("_root.circle" +
                  _root.counter, _yscale, 100-
                  (2*_root.counter));

                _root.counter = _root.counter +
                  1;
        }
}
```

5. Test the movie to see the result.

spinner2.fla

Duplicating with Purpose: Example 2

1. Open the file `spinner2.fla`. This also has a single frame action of `counter = 1`.

2. Click on the square and enter this code into its Object Actions panel:

```
onClipEvent(enterFrame)
{
        if(this._name == "square" && _root.counter <
          180)
        {
                        this.duplicateMovieClip
                          ("square"+ _root.counter,
                          _root.counter);
                        setProperty("_root.square"+
                          _root.counter, _rotation,
                          _root.counter*2);

                        _root.counter = _root.counter +
                          1;

        }
}
```

3. Test the movie. It runs slowly, but it's worth it.

whatisthatthing.fla

Duplicating with Purpose: Example 3

1. Open the file `whatisthatthing.fla`.
2. Open up the sphere symbol from the symbol list.
3. Notice that this movie clip is a simple circle with a gradient. There are two aspects that change during its shape tweens: its size shrinks and the tint changes. That's it.
4. Go back to the main scene.
5. Notice the ever-present frame action `counter = 1;`.
6. Click on the sphere (note its instance name is "`sphere0`", not "`sphere`") and enter the following code:

```
onClipEvent(enterFrame)
{
        if(this._name == "sphere0" && _root.counter
          <50)
        {

                        this.duplicateMovieClip(
                          "sphere"+ _root.counter,
                          _root.counter);

                        // determine x-direction
                          movement
                        xOrig = getProperty
                          ("_root.sphere" +
                          (_root.counter-1),_x);
                        xDiam = getProperty
                          ("_root.sphere" +
                          (_root.counter-1), _xscale);
                        xRandom = Math.random()*
                          (xDiam/5);
                        xDirection = Math.random();
                        if(xDirection < .5)
                        {
                                        xRandom = xRandom *
                                          -1;
                        }
```

```
// determine y-direction
  movement
yOrig = getProperty("_root.
  sphere" + (_root.counter-1),
  _y);
yDiam = getProperty
  ("_root.sphere" +
  (_root.counter-1), _yscale);
yRandom = Math.random()*
  (yDiam/5);
yDirection = Math.random();
if(yDirection < .5)
{
            yRandom = yRandom *
               -1;
}

// alter properties
setProperty("_root.sphere" +
  _root.counter, _x, xOrig +
  xRandom);
setProperty("_root.sphere" +
  _root.counter, _y, yOrig +
  yRandom);
setProperty("_root.sphere" +
  _root.counter, _xscale, 100-
  (_root.counter*2));
setProperty("_root.sphere" +
  _root.counter, _yscale, 100-
  (_root.counter*2));

_root.counter = _root.counter +
  1;

            }
      }
```

7. Test the movie.

duplicate2.fla

Loading Movies

1. Open duplicate2.fla.
2. Click on the ball and open its Object Actions panel.
3. Enter this code:

```
onClipEvent(mouseUp)
{
        if(this._name == "ball")
        {

                this.duplicateMovieClip("ball" +
                    _root.counter, _root.counter);
                setProperty("_root.ball" +
                    _root.counter, _x,  Math.ran-
                    dom() * 500);
                setProperty("_root.ball" +
                    _root.counter, _y,  Math.ran-
                    dom() * 400);
                if(_root.counter > 10)
                {
                        removeMovieClip
                            ("_root.ball" +
                            (_root.counter-
                            10));
                }

                if(_root.counter == 20)
                {
                        loadMovie("what
                            isthatthing_done
                            .swf", 1);
                }

                _root.counter = _root.counter +
                    1;

        }
}
```

4. Test the movie and click about 25 times.

duplicate2.fla

Unloading Movies

1. Change

```
loadMovie("whatisthatthing_done.swf", 0);
```

back to

```
loadMovie("whatisthatthing_done.swf", 1);
```

2. Add another if statement, like so:

```
onClipEvent(mouseUp)
{
        if(this._name == "ball")
        {

                this.duplicateMovieClip("ball" +
                  _root.counter, _root.counter);
                setProperty("_root.ball" +
                  _root.counter, _x,  Math.ran-
                  dom() * 500);
                setProperty("_root.ball" +
                  _root.counter, _y,  Math.ran-
                  dom() * 400);
                if(_root.counter > 10)
                {
                           removeMovieClip
                              ("_root.ball" +
                  (_root.counter-10));
                }

                if(_root.counter == 20)
                {
                           loadMovie("what
                              isthatthing_
                              done.swf", 1);
                }
                else if(_root.counter == 25)
                {
                           unloadMovie(_level1);
                }
```

```
                _root.counter = _root.counter +
                   1;
         }
      }
```

3. Test the movie, and click until the gray thing disappears.

Attaching Movie Clips

Suppose you have three movie clips: A, B, and C.

- You can attach movie clip B to movie clip A. A becomes the parent movie clip and B is the child.
- When B is attached to A, what you do to A happens to B automatically.
- You can also attach movie clip C to movie clip B.
- Anything you do to movie clip C happens only to movie clip C.
- Anything you do to movie clip B happens to clips B and C.
- Anything you do to movie clip A happens to clips A, B, and C.
- This linking of properties from parent to child is called *inheritance*.

Notes:

_____

_____

_____

_____

_____

_____

_____

_____

_____

_____

attachMovie()

Syntax

```
someMovieClip.attachMovie( nameOfInstance, newName, depth)
```

frank1.fla

Dragging the Body in the Frank Movie

1. Open `frank1.fla`.
2. Note that this movie uses a mask layer over the body layer. That doesn't affect our actions, but we haven't used one yet, so you should be aware of it.
3. Click on the large `body` object (named *body* in the Instance panel).
4. Enter this code:

```
onClipEvent(mouseDown)
{
        if((_root._xmouse > 20) &&
(_root._xmouse < 588) &&
                        (_root._ymouse > 200) &&
(_root._ymouse < 592))
            {
                        startDrag(this, false, 20, 200,
                            588, 592);
            }
}

onClipEvent(mouseUp)
{
        stopDrag();
}
```

5. Test the movie.

frank1.fla

Attaching the Head

1. In order for a movie clip to be attached to another, it has to be linked and named in a special way. We'll link the "head" symbol, and then enter some code.
2. Open the Library.
3. Click on the "head" symbol.
4. Under the Options menu, go to Linkage....
5. Click Export this symbol.
6. In the Identifier text field, enter "head".
7. Click OK.
8. Back in the Flash movie, click on the tiny head.
9. Enter this code:

```
onClipEvent(mouseDown)
{
        // see if user clicked on this image
        bounds = this.getBounds(_root);

        // see if the user clicked inside the head
        if((_root._xmouse <= bounds.xMax) &&
(_root._xmouse >= bounds.xMin) &&
                (_root._ymouse <= bounds.yMax)
&&
(_root._ymouse >= bounds.yMin))
        {
                        //attach the head
                        _root.body.attachMovie
                          ("head","head", 15);
                        //position the head
                        _root.body.head._y = -160;
        }
}
```

10. Test the movie.

frank1.fla

Attaching the Hand

1. Open the Library, if it isn't already open.
2. Click on the "hand" symbol.
3. Choose Linkage... from the Options menu.
4. Choose Export this symbol.
5. Enter "hand" for Identifier.
6. Click OK.
7. Back in your Flash movie, click on the hand and open its Object Actions panel.
8. Enter this code:

```
onClipEvent(mouseDown)
{
        // see if user clicked on this image
        bounds = this.getBounds(_root);


        // see if the user clicked inside the hand
        if((_root._xmouse <= bounds.xMax) &&
(_root._xmouse >= bounds.xMin) &&
                (_root._ymouse <= bounds.yMax)
                  &&
(_root._ymouse >= bounds.yMin))
        {
                        //attach the hand
                        _root.body.attachMovie
                          ("hand","hand", 3);

                        //position the hand
                        _root.body.hand._y = -96;
                        _root.body.hand._x = 207;
                        _root.body.hand._rotation = -22;
        }
}
```

9. Test the movie. Click on the head and the hand, and drag everything around.

frank1.fla

Attaching the Left Foot

1. Open the Library, if it isn't already open.
2. Click on the `mc_foot_left` symbol.
3. Choose Linkage... from the Options menu.
4. Choose Export this symbol.
5. Enter "`leftFoot`" as the Identifier.
6. Click OK.
7. Back in your Flash movie, click on the small left foot and open its Object Actions panel.
8. Enter this code:

```
onClipEvent (mouseDown)
{
                // see if user clicked on this image
                bounds = this.getBounds(_root);

                // see if the user clicked inside the
                  leftFoot
                if((_root._xmouse <= bounds.xMax) &&
(_root._xmouse >= bounds.xMin) &&
                         (_root._ymouse <=
                           bounds.yMax) &&
(_root._ymouse >= bounds.yMin))
                {
                         //attach the leftFoot
                _root.body.legs.attachMovie("left
                  Foot","leftFoot",
                  3);

                         //position the leftFoot
                         _root.body.legs.left
                           Foot._x = -68;
                         _root.body.legs.left
                           Foot._y = 83;

                }

        }
```

9. Test the movie. Note that you have to add the legs before you add the left foot. Until you add the legs, the foot has nothing to attach to, so nothing happens. It's a little surprising no error message appears, but that's how Flash 5 works.

space_game.fla

Tweak Frank Files

The files containing the code from the Tweak Frank project are named as follows:

- Frame Action   =   `list3-8.txt`
- Big Body Object   =   `list3-9.txt`
- Head   =   `list3-10.txt`
- Right Bolt   =   `list3-11.txt`
- Left Bolt   =   `list3-12.txt`
- Left Arm   =   `list3-13.txt`
- Pants   =   `list3-14.txt`
- Left Foot   =   `list3-15.txt`
- Right Foot   =   `list3-16.txt`
- Body—Tweak Box   =   `list3-17.txt`
- Pants—Tweak Box   =   `list3-18.txt`

Notes:

_____

_____

_____

_____

_____

_____

_____

Tweak Frank

Frame Action

```
bodyFade = false;
legsFade = false;
```

Tweak Frank

Right Bolt

```
onClipEvent(mouseDown)
{
        // see if user clicked on this image
        bounds = this.getBounds(_root);

        // see if the user clicked inside the rightBolt
        if((_root._xmouse <= bounds.xMax) &&
                    (_root._xmouse >= bounds.xMin) &&
                    (_root._ymouse <= bounds.yMax) &&
                    (_root._ymouse >= bounds.yMin))
        {
                //attach the rightBolt
            _root.body.attachMovie("rightBolt","right
              Bolt",14);

                //position the rightBolt
                _root.body.rightBolt._x = 100;
                _root.body.rightBolt._y = -128;
        }
}
```

Tweak Frank

Left Bolt

```
onClipEvent(mouseDown)
{
        // see if user clicked on this image
        bounds = this.getBounds(_root);

        // see if the user clicked inside the leftBolt
        if((_root._xmouse <= bounds.xMax) &&
                    (_root._xmouse >= bounds.xMin) &&
                    (_root._ymouse <= bounds.yMax) &&
                    (_root._ymouse >= bounds.yMin))
        {
                    //attach the leftBolt
                    _root.body.attachMovie
                      ("leftBolt","leftBolt",13);
                    //position the leftBolt
                    _root.body.leftBolt._x = -94;
                    _root.body.leftBolt._y = -121;
        }
}
```

Tweak Frank

Left Arm

```
onClipEvent(mouseDown)
{
        // see if user clicked on this image
        bounds = this.getBounds(_root);

        // see if the user clicked inside the arm
        if((_root._xmouse <= bounds.xMax) &&
                    (_root._xmouse >= bounds.xMin) &&
                    (_root._ymouse <= bounds.yMax) &&
                    (_root._ymouse >= bounds.yMin))
        {
                    //attach the arm
                    _root.body.attachMovie("arm","arm",
                      6);

                    //position the arm
                    _root.body.arm._y = -17;
                    _root.body.arm._x = -191;
        }
}
```

Tweak Frank

Pants

```
onClipEvent(mouseDown)
{
        // see if user clicked on this image
        bounds = this.getBounds(_root);

        // see if the user clicked inside the legs
        if((_root._xmouse <= bounds.xMax) &&
                    (_root._xmouse >= bounds.xMin) &&
                    (_root._ymouse <= bounds.yMax) &&
                    (_root._ymouse >= bounds.yMin))
        {
                    //attach the legs
                    _root.body.attachMovie("legs","legs",
                      10);

                    //position the legs
                    _root.body.legs._y = 87;
        }
}
```

Tweak Frank

Right Foot

```
onClipEvent(mouseDown)
{
        // see if user clicked on this image
        bounds = this.getBounds(_root);

        // see if the user clicked inside the rightFoot
        if((_root._xmouse <= bounds.xMax) &&
                    (_root._xmouse >= bounds.xMin) &&
                    (_root._ymouse <= bounds.yMax) &&
                    (_root._ymouse >= bounds.yMin))
        {
                //attach the rightFoot
_root.body.legs.attachMovie("rightFoot","right
    Foot",4);

                //position the rightFoot
                _root.body.legs.rightFoot._x = 102;
                _root.body.legs.rightFoot._y = 86;
        }
}
```

Tweak Frank

Body—Tweak Box

```
onClipEvent(mouseDown)
{
        // see if user clicked on this image
        bounds = this.getBounds(_root);

        // see if the user clicked inside the body
        if((_root._xmouse <= bounds.xMax) &&
                   (_root._xmouse >= bounds.xMin) &&
                   (_root._ymouse <= bounds.yMax) &&
                   (_root._ymouse >= bounds.yMin))
        {
                // tweak body
                if(_root.bodyFade)
                {
                        _root.body._alpha = 100;
                        _root.bodyFade = false;
                }
                else
                {
                        _root.body._alpha = 30;
                        _root.bodyFade = true;
                }
        }
}
```

Tweak Frank

Pants—Tweak Box

```
onClipEvent(mouseDown)
{
        // see if user clicked on this image
        bounds = this.getBounds(_root);

        // see if the user clicked inside the legs
        if((_root._xmouse <= bounds.xMax) &&
                (_root._xmouse >= bounds.xMin) &&
                (_root._ymouse <= bounds.yMax) &&
                (_root._ymouse >= bounds.yMin))
        {
                // tweak legs
                if(_root.legsFade)
                {
                        _root.body.legs._alpha =
                          100;
                        _root.legsFade = false;
                }
                else
                {
                        _root.body.legs._alpha =
                          30;
                        _root.legsFade = true;
                }
        }
}
```

Lesson 3.3

Explore the Movie Explorer

The Movie Explorer

The Movie Explorer dissects your movie into all of its different parts: frames, scenes, layers, sounds, actions, symbols, text, and so on. It looks like this:

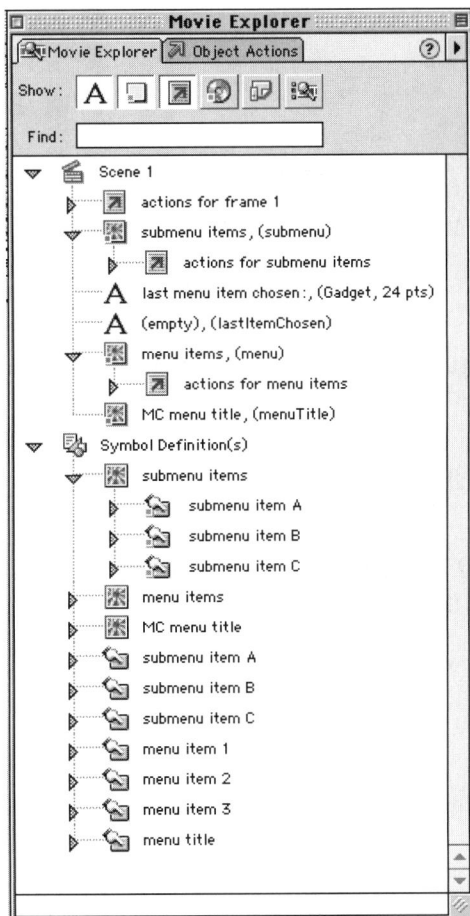

Lecture 4

Serious Interactivity

Objectives

- Link to Other Web Pages with Your Flash Movie

- Receive Data from Other Pages with Your Flash Movie

- Send Variables with `loadVariables`

- Access JavaScript or Control the Flash Player with FSCommand

Lesson 4.1

Link to Other Web Pages with Your Flash Movie

linking1.fla

Linking to the Outside World

1. Open the file `linking1.fla`, which you copied to your hard drive at the start of this lecture.
2. Click on the arrow-in-a-circle button, shown here, and open its Object Actions panel.
3. Enter this code:
   ```
   on(release)
   {
     getURL("linking_page1.html")
   }
   ```
4. File → Publish.
5. Copy `linking_page1.html` from the example files to wherever your exported Flash file is.
6. Open the resulting HTML file, `linking1.html`, in your browser of choice and click on the button.

Note that:
```
getURL("linking_page1.html","_blank")
```
Is the same as:
```
<a href="linking_page1.html" target="_blank">
```

Linking to Web Pages

The target can be the name of a window, or one of several reserved words:

- `_blank` opens a new window.
- `_self` opens the new page in the current window.
- `_top` opens the page in the top-level frame in the current window. In other words, it removes all the frames and fills the browser with the new page.
- `_parent` opens the page in next higher-level frame in the current window.

Notes:

_____

_____

_____

_____

_____

_____

_____

_____

_____

_____

_____

linking1.fla

Sending Variables

1. Open the file `linking1.fla`, if it isn't already open.
2. Click on the frame in the actions layer, and open the Frame Actions panel.
3. Enter this code:
   ```
   shirt = "red";
   ```
4. Click on the button and open its Object Actions panel.
5. Change the code to:
   ```
   on(release)
   {
     pants = "blue";
     getURL("linking_page1.html", "_blank", "get");
   }
   ```
6. Save and publish the file. (Note that on a Windows machine, the file must be loaded to a Web server for the query string to appear.) Open the page in a browser, click on the button, and notice the URL. As shown here, it should end with:
   ```
   linking_page1.html?shirt=red&pants=blue.
   ```

Linking to Web Pages

get

- The third attribute in the getURL action determines whether any existing variables are sent via the get method (in the URL) or the post method (in a separate HTTP header).
- Notice that the variables are those attached to the object (the button) and global variables. Variables attached to other movie clips are not sent.
- For example, if we had another movie clip in the movie that contained a variable called "shoes", that variable would not be sent by the button's getURL action.
- Flash will always view the second attribute as a target assignment:
```
on(release)
{
  pants = "blue";
  getURL("linking_page1.html", "_blank", "get");
}
```
- If your code is:
```
getURL("linking_page1.html", "get");
```

Flash will look for a browser window called "get". If Flash doesn't find one, it will open a new browser window. And since Flash thought "get" was the name of a browser window, it won't try to send any variables.

- If you want to send variables and stay in the same browser window, use this code:
```
getURL("linking_page1.html", "_self", "get");
```
- As an alternative, you can replace "_self" with an empty string:
```
getURL("linking_page1.html", "", "get");
```
- Instead of linking to an HMTL page, you can send variables to any file:
```
getURL("validate_form.php", "_self",
      "post");
```

or:

```
getURL("update_resume.cfm", "_self",
      "post");
```

Transparent Buttons

- A transparent button can be placed over anything: text, parts of a movie clip, and so on. It can make some functionality much easier to implement.
- An example would be to place a few buttons over selected words in a paragraph of text. Those buttons could act as links. You can then change the text as much as you would like and not have to create separate text buttons for the words that are links.
- You can also have a single invisible button symbol that can be used over and over simply by changing the scale and size once it's on the stage.

Notes:

_____

_____

_____

_____

_____

_____

_____

_____

_____

_____

_____

Lesson 4.2

Receive Data from Other Pages with Your Flash Movie

quotes.txt

Pulling Data from a Text File

1. Open the text file `quotes.txt`, which you copied to your hard drive at the start of this lecture. Note that it has only one line:
   ```
   quote=hi+there!
   ```
2. Open the file `quotes1.fla`.
3. Note that there are two elements in this movie: some static text and some dynamic text. The static text is the blue Quote of the Day.

   The dynamic text is a large, multi-line block of text named "`quote`".
4. Click in the frame in the actions layer and open its Frame Actions panel.
5. Enter this code:
   ```
   loadVariables("quotes.txt", _root)
   ```
6. Test the movie. "hi there!" should appear almost as soon as the movie starts playing.

Receiving Data

loadVariables and Subdomains

The first attribute of `loadVariables` determines which file Flash should load the variables from.

```
loadVariables("quotes.txt", _root)
```

This file can live anywhere in the same subdomain as the Flash movie. For example:

DOMAIN	*SUBDOMAIN*
www.wire-man.com	wire-man.com
camel.llama.wire-man.com	llama.wire-man.com
wire-man.com	wire-man.com

Here's the rule: If the domain has only two components, the subdomain is the same as the domain. If the domain has more than two components, then remove the last level to find the subdomain.

The second attribute of `loadVariables` tells Flash where to place the variable(s) that are in the file.

```
loadVariables("quotes.txt", _root)
```

You can place variables in the root level, in a specific movie clip, or on a level.

Lesson 4.3

Send Variables with loadVariables

Sending Variables with loadVariables

```
loadVariables(filename, target, "get"/"post");
```

- That's it—just the "get"/"post" part. That'll send all available variables to the indicated file.

Notes:

_____

_____

_____

_____

_____

_____

_____

_____

_____

_____

_____

Formatting the Variables so Flash Can Read Them

```
variable1=value1&variable2=value2&variable3=value3
```

- If there are spaces in one of the values, replace the space with a plus sign, like this:

```
variable1=value1&variable2=value2&variable3=value3
quote1=Wherever+you+go,+there+you+are.&address-
Num=180&suite=2
```

Notes:

_____

_____

_____

_____

_____

_____

_____

_____

_____

_____

_____

_____

Lesson 4.4

Control the Standalone Flash Player with FSCommand

javascript1.fla

Control the Standalone Flash Player with FSCommand

1. Open `javascript1.fla`, which is among the files you copied to your hard drive for this lecture.
2. Click on the frame in the actions layer and open its Frame actions layer.
3. Enter this code:
   ```
   fscommand("allowscale", "true");
   ```
4. Test the movie. Notice that as you resize the window, the movie resizes as well, as shown here.
5. Go back to the Flash movie.
6. Change the code to this:
   ```
   fscommand("allowscale", "false");
   ```
7. Test the movie. Notice, that as you resize the window, the movie doesn't resize.

Lecture 5

Flash and XML

Objectives

- Examine and Explain XML

- Read an Imported XML Document

- Create XML from Scratch

Lesson 5.1

Examine and Explain XML

XML Example

"Soupy Sales: Godfather of the Sitcom"

```
<xml>
<article type="magazine">
        <headline>Soupy Sales</headline>
        <subhead>Godfather of the Sitcom</subhead>
        <byline>
                    <author>
                                    <firstName>Irving
                                    </firstname>
                                    <lastName>Archbite
                                    </lastname>
                    </author>
        </byline>
        <body>Blah blah blah</body>
</article>
</xml>
```

XML: Markup Language

- Just as HTML is Hypertext Markup Language, XML stands for eXtensible Markup Language.
- Both XML and HTML come from the same parent, SGML.

Another Example: A String and a Small Array

```
<xml>
  <string text="hi there" />
  <array>
        <element>56</element>
        <element>75</element>
        <element>3</element>
  </array>
</xml>
```

All elements in XML must be closed:

`<tag>` must have a `</tag>`

Exception:
`<tag />`

is only used for single-element nodes.

Notes:

_____

_____

_____

_____

Roll Your Own XML

You decide how to mark up your XML. This is perfectly valid XML:

```
<xml>
  <dogbite>arrf arf arf!</dogbite>
  <cat breed="Siamese">meow meow. Hiss!</cat>
  <owner>Bad Barney! Bad!</owner>
</xml>
```

Lesson 5.2

Read an Imported XML Document

Read an Imported XML Document

```
<cat breed="siamese">meow meow. Hiss!!</cat>
```

- breed is an *attribute* of the <cat> node
- meow meow. Hiss!! is a *text node* within the <cat> node = a *child node* of <cat>.

Notes:

_____

_____

_____

_____

_____

_____

_____

_____

_____

_____

_____

The XML Object

The Screenplay Example

Here's what the screenplay example looks like:

```
<screenplay title="Three Days of the Condor">
        <author>Lorenzo Semple, Jr.</author>
        <author>David Rayfiel</author>
        <character type="main">Turner</character>
        <character type="major">Kathy</character>
        <character type="major">Higgins</character>
        <character type="major">Jobert</character>
        <character type="major">Mr. Wabash</character>

        <act number="1">
                <dramaticNeed>Who's trying to kill
                  Turner and why?</dramaticNeed>
                <plotPoint>Turner returns from lunch
                  to find everyone in his bookish
                  CIA office dead.</plotPoint>
        </act>

        <act number="2">
                <obstacle description="Turner tries
                  to get to a safe place">
                          <sequence>Turner calls
                            HQ.</sequence>
                          <sequence>Turner is
                            betrayed in
                            alley.</sequence>
                </obstacle>
                <obstacle description="Mailman/
                  assassin attacks Turner">
                          <sequence>Turner and
                            mailman fight. Turner
                            wins.</sequence>
                </obstacle>
                <plotPoint>Turner captures head CIA
                  deputy and becomes attacker
                  instead of victim.</plotPoint>
        </act>
```

```
<act number="3">
                <resolution>Turner finds the man who
                   ordered the murders, and why they
                   were done.</resolution>
                <tagScene>Turner gives his story to
                   the NY Times, and wonders if they
                   will print it.</tagScene>
     </act>

</screenplay>
```

However, Flash can't read XML documents that have carriage returns or extra spaces (probably a bug that will be fixed). The Flash file needs to look like this:

```
<screenplay title="Three Days of the
Condor"><author>Lorenzo Semple, Jr.</
author><author>David Rayfiel</author><character
type="main">Turner</character><character
type="major">Kathy</character><character
type="major">Higgins</character><character
type="major">Jobert</character><character type="major">Mr.
Wabash</character><act num-

ber="1"><dramaticNeed>Who's trying to kill Turner and
why?</dramaticNeed><plotPoint>Turner returns from
lunch to find everyone in his bookish CIA office

dead.</plotPoint></act><act number="2"><obstacle

description="Turner tries to get to a safe place">
<sequence>Turner calls HQ.</sequence><sequence>
Turner is betrayed in alley.</sequence></obstacle>
<obstacle description="Mailman/assassin attacks
Turner"><sequence>Turner and mailman

fight. Turner wins.</sequence></obstacle><plot-Point>
Turner captures head CIA deputy and becomes attacker
instead of victim.</plotPoint></act><act number="3">
<resolution>Turner finds the man who ordered the
murders, and why they were done.</resolu-
```

```
tion><tagScene>Turner gives his story to the NY Times,and
wonders if they will print it.</tagScene></act></screen-
play>
```

Using Flash to Read Through an XML Document

1. Create a folder somewhere on your hard drive called *Flash &* *XML*.
2. Copy `screenplay_space.xml` to that folder.
3. Open Flash and create a new file called `xml1.fla`. Save this file to the Flash & XML folder.
4. Go back to the `xml1_done.fla` file in Flash.
5. Click on the single frame on layer 1 and open its Frame Actions panel.
6. Enter this code:
   ```
   //create XML object
   screenplayXML = new XML();

   // load external file into XML object
   screenplayXML.load("screenplay_space.xml");

   // when loading is complete, go to a special function
   screenplayXML.onLoad = loadedXML;

   function loadedXML()
   {
           trace("the XML object is loaded")
   }
   ```
7. Test the movie. A blank Flash player should appear, along with the output window, with the expected message.

Dissecting the Screenplay

```
<screenplay title="Three Days of the Condor">
        <author>Lorenzo Semple, Jr.</author>
        <author>David Rayfiel</author>
        …
</screenplay>
```

The way to access the first child node of an XML object is

```
xmlObj.firstChild
```

Dissecting the Screenplay (cont)

```
<author>Lorenzo Semple, Jr.</author>
<author>David Rayfiel</author>
```

- It may appear that <author> nodes have no more child nodes. However, the text Lorenzo Semple, Jr. is a special kind of node, called a text node, and it can be a child node as well.

Notes:

_____

_____

_____

_____

_____

_____

_____

_____

_____

_____

_____

_____

XML Child Nodes

```
author1Node.firstChild = author1Name
```

- author1Name is the first child of author1Node
  allText.firstChild.firstChild

is the same as:

```
author1Node.firstChild
```

is the same as:

```
author1Name
```

author1Name is the child of author1Node and the grandchild of allText.

And finally,

```
screenplayXML.firstChild.firstChild.firstChild
```

is the same as:

```
allText.firstChild.firstChild
```

is the same as:

```
author1Node.firstChild
```

is the same as:

```
author1Name
```

```
screenplayXML.firstChild.firstChild.firstChild
  allText.firstChild.firstChild
  author1Node.firstChild
  author1Name
```

All point to the same place in the XML. They all have the same and equal value.

allText **Node**

Remember, the allText node is:

```
<screenplay title=ÅgThree Days of the CondorÅh>
  Åceverything elseÅc
</screenplay>
```

The code looks for the attribute named title (because a node can have more than one attribute) and places that value in movieTitle, which is then displayed.

Notes:

_____

_____

_____

_____

_____

_____

_____

_____

_____

_____

Structure of the Screenplay

```
<screenplay title="Three Days of the Condor">
        <author>…author>
        <author>…</author>
        <character type="main">…</character>
        <character type="major">…</character>
        <character type="major">…</character>
        <character type="major">…</character>
        <character type="major">…</character>
        <act number="1">…</act>
        <act number="2">…</act>
        <act number="3">…</act>
</screenplay>
```

- We may not know how many authors, characters, or acts this screenplay may have when itÅfs first loaded.
- We can find this out by using a few new methods and properties: `childNodes`, `nodeName`, and `nextSibling`.

Notes:

_____

_____

_____

_____

_____

_____

_____

_____

xml1.fla

Here's all of the code for the screenplay example (also found in
list5-1.txt):

```
//create XML object
screenplayXML = new XML();

// load external file into XML object
screenplayXML.load("screenplay_space.xml");

// when loading is complete, go to a special function
screenplayXML.onLoad = loadedXML;

function loadedXML()
{
        // set sub-objects
        allText = screenplayXML.firstChild;
        c = allText.firstChild;

        //dissect
        movieTitle = allText.attributes.title
        trace(movieTitle)

        // finding number of child nodes
        allTextChildren = allText.childNodes;
        numChildren = allTextChildren.length;

        for(i=0; i<numChildren; i++)
        {
                cNodeStr = c.firstChild.
                  nodeValue.toString();

                // find number of authors
                if(c.nodeName == "author")
                {
                                if(cNodeStr.indexOf
                                  ("Lorenzo") != -1)
                                {

c.firstChild.nodeValue = "Clark
                                              Kent";
```

```
                }
                authorName = c.firstChild;
                trace("author: " + authorName);
        }
        else if(c.nodeName == "character")
        {
                if(cNodeStr.indexOf("Wabash") != -1)
                {
                        d = c.previousSibling;
                        c.removeNode();
                        c = d;
                }
                else
                {
                        typeChar = c.attrib-
                          utes.type;
                        characterName =
                          c.firstChild.node
                          Value;
                        trace("character: " +
                          typeChar + ": " +
                          characterName);
                }
        }
        else if(c.nodeName == "act")
        {
                actNum = c.attributes.number
                trace("act" + actNum);
        }

                c = c.nextSibling;
        }
}
```

Lesson 5.3

Create XML from Scratch

Creating XML

Entire Screenplay Example (`list5-2.txt`

```
// create XML object
screenplayXML = new XML();

// create screenplay element/node
screenElement = screenplayXML.createElement("screenplay");

// place the screenplay element
screenplayXML.appendChild(screenElement);
screenElement.attributes.title = "Three Days of the
Condor";

//create first author element
authorElement = screenplayXML.createElement("author");
authorName = screenplayXML.createTextNode("Lorenzo Semple,
Jr.")

//place first author element
screenElement.appendChild(authorElement);
authorElement.appendChild(authorName);

// create and place second author element
authorElem2 = authorElement.cloneNode(true);
screenElement.appendChild(authorElem2);
authorElem2.firstChild.nodeValue = "David Rayfiel";

//create a character element
charElement = screenplayXML.createElement("character");
charName = screenplayXML.createTextNode("Turner");

//place main character element
screenElement.appendChild(charElement);
charElement.appendChild(charName);
charElement.attributes.type = "main";
```

```
//create remaining character elements
charElement2 = charElement.cloneNode(true);
charElement2.attributes.type = "major";
charElement2.firstChild.nodeValue = "Kathy";

charElement3 = charElement2.cloneNode(true);
charElement3.firstChild.nodeValue = "Higgins";

charElement4 = charElement2.cloneNode(true);
charElement4.firstChild.nodeValue = "Jobert";

charElement5 = charElement2.cloneNode(true);
charElement5.firstChild.nodeValue = "Mr. Wabash";

// place character elements
screenElement.appendChild(charElement2);
screenElement.appendChild(charElement3);
screenElement.appendChild(charElement4);
screenElement.appendChild(charElement5);

//create the acts
actElement = screenplayXML.createElement("act");
actElement.attributes.number = "1";

actElement2 = actElement.cloneNode(true);
actElement2.attributes.number = "2";

actElement3 = actElement.cloneNode(true);
actElement3.attributes.number = "3";

//place the acts
screenElement.appendChild(actElement);
screenElement.appendChild(actElement2);
screenElement.appendChild(actElement3);

//create act 1 elements
dramaNeedElement = screenplayXML.createElement("dramatic-
Need");
dramaNeedText = screenplayXML.createTextNode("Who's trying
to kill Turner and why?")
plotPointElement = screenplayXML.createElement("plot-
Point");
plotPointText = screenplayXML.createTextNode("Turner re-
turns from lunch to find everyone in his bookish CIA of-
fice dead");
```

```
//place act 1 elements
actElement.appendChild(dramaNeedElement);
actElement.appendChild(plotPointElement);
dramaNeedElement.appendChild(dramaNeedText);
plotPointElement.appendChild(plotPointText);

//create act 2 elements
obstacleElement1 = screenplayXML.createElement
("obstacle");
obstacleElement1.attributes.description = "Turner tries to
get to a safe place"

obstacleElement2 = obstacleElement1.cloneNode(true)
obstacleElement2.attributes.description = "Mailman/assas-
sin attacks Turner";

sequenceElement1 = screenplayXML.createElement("se-
quence");
sequenceText1 = screenplayXML.createTextNode("Turner calls
HQ");
sequenceElement1.appendChild(sequenceText1);

sequenceElement2 = sequenceElement1.cloneNode(true);
sequenceElement2.firstChild.nodeValue = "Turner is
betrayed in alley"

sequenceElement3 = sequenceElement1.cloneNode(true);
sequenceElement3.firstChild.nodeValue = "Turner and
mailman fight. Turner wins";

plotPointElement2 = plotPointElement.cloneNode(true);
plotPointElement2.firstChild.nodeValue = "Turner captures
head CIA deputy and becomes attacker instead of victim";

//place act 2 elements
actElement2.appendChild(obstacleElement1);
actElement2.appendChild(obstacleElement2);
actElement2.appendChild(plotPointElement2);

obstacleElement1.appendChild(sequenceElement1);
obstacleElement1.appendChild(sequenceElement2);
obstacleElement2.appendChild(sequenceElement3);
```

```
// create act 3 elements
resolutionElement = screenplayXML.createElement
("resolution");
tagElement = screenplayXML.createElement("tagScene");

resolutionText = screenplayXML.createTextNode("Turner
finds the man who ordered the murders, and why they were
done");
tagSceneText = screenplayXML.createTextNode("Turner gives
his story to the NY Times, and wonders if they will print
it");

//place act 3 elements
actElement3.appendChild(resolutionElement);
actElement3.appendChild(tagElement);

resolutionElement.appendChild(resolutionText);
tagElement.appendChild(tagSceneText);

// display
trace(screenplayXML.firstChild)
```

Lecture 6

Troubleshooting ActionScript

Objectives

- Watch and Alter Certain Parts of Your Movie with the Debugger Window

- Troubleshoot Easily Using Comments

- Test Your Movie by Listing Objects and Variables

Lesson 6.1

Watch and Alter Certain Parts of Your Movie with the Debugger Window

The Debugger Window

With the Debugger window, you can:

- Watch the values of all the variables in the movie and see how they change while the movie plays.
- Change some properties of movie clips while they play.
- Change the values of variables.
- Create a list of watched variables (helpful if you have a lot of variables but are curious about only a few of them).
- Change the values of watched variables.

Notes:

_____

_____

_____

_____

_____

_____

_____

pudgy_done.fla

Opening the Debugging Window

1. Open the file pudgy_done.fla.
2. Control → Debug Movie.
   The movie and the Debugger window will appear.
   There's supposed to be some useful information in that window.
3. Close the Debugger window.
4. Control-click (Mac users) or right-click (Windows folk) on the movie and choose Debugger from the contextual menu that pops up.

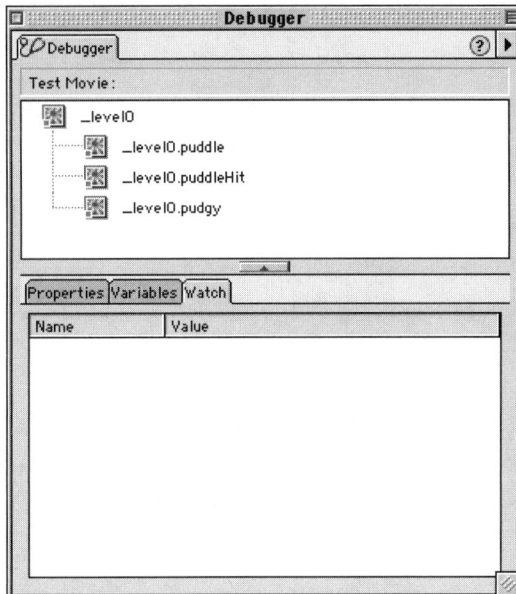

5. A new Debugger window should appear, like this:

6. Notice that all the symbols in the movie are listed in the Display window, preceded by `_level0` or possibly by `_root`. Click on the pudgy instance (`_level0.pudgy`).

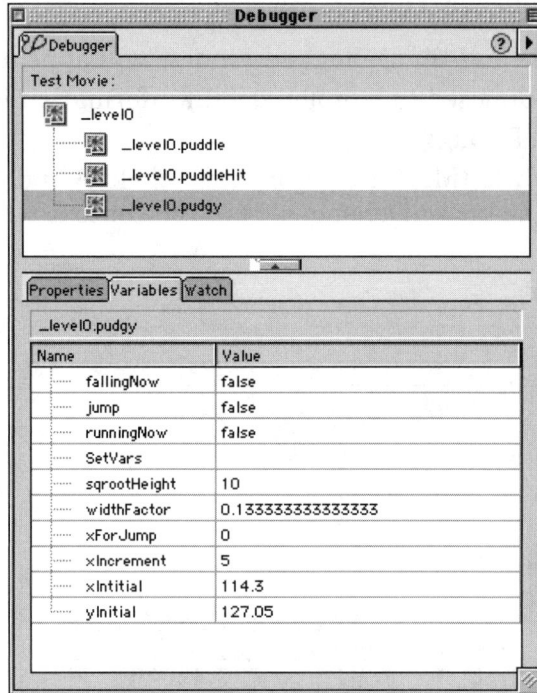

Name	Value
fallingNow	false
jump	false
runningNow	false
SetVars	
sqrootHeight	10
widthFactor	0.133333333333333
xForJump	0
xIncrement	5
xIntitial	114.3
yInitial	127.05

7. Click on the Variables tab, shown here:

8. Click back on the movie and start pressing arrow keys (except the down arrow—that one doesn't do anything).

pudgy_done.fla

Watching Variables

1. Play the Pudgy game for a few seconds by pressing the arrow keys (this initializes some variables).
2. Control-click (Mac) or right-click (Windows) on `fallingNow` in the `_level0.pudgy` variable list (click on the Variables tab if it isn't highlighted).
3. Choose Watch. It's the only option. Note that a blue dot appears next to the variable name.
4. Do the same for `jump`, `leftArrowDown`, `rightArrowDown`, andrunningNow.
5. Click on the Watch tab. It should look something like this:

6. Notice something odd? The variables are listed using what's called *slash syntax* (as opposed to the dot syntax Flash 5 uses). Slash syntax is left over from Flash 4, so if you've used Flash before, this is probably familiar to you. If not, don't worry: the meaning is the same. `_level0/pudgy:jump` is the same thing as `_level0.pudgy.jump`. In slash syntax, levels of hierarchy are denoted by slashes and variables are preceded by a colon.
7. Click back on the movie and start using the arrow keys again. Notice how the variables change as you move Pudgy about the screen.

pudgy_done.fla

Changing Properties

1. Click on `_level0.pudgy` in the Debugger window's display list.
2. Click on the Properties tab.
3. Try double-clicking some of the property values and changing them. The ones you can change are colored black. The others are gray.
4. Double-click the value next to `_alpha`. Enter50 and press Enter.
5. Double-click the value next to `_xscale`. Enter100 and press Enter.
6. Double-click the value next to `_yscale`. Enter200 and press Enter.
7. Double-click the value next to `_y`. Enter50 and press Enter.

You get the idea. The tweaked movie should look something like this:

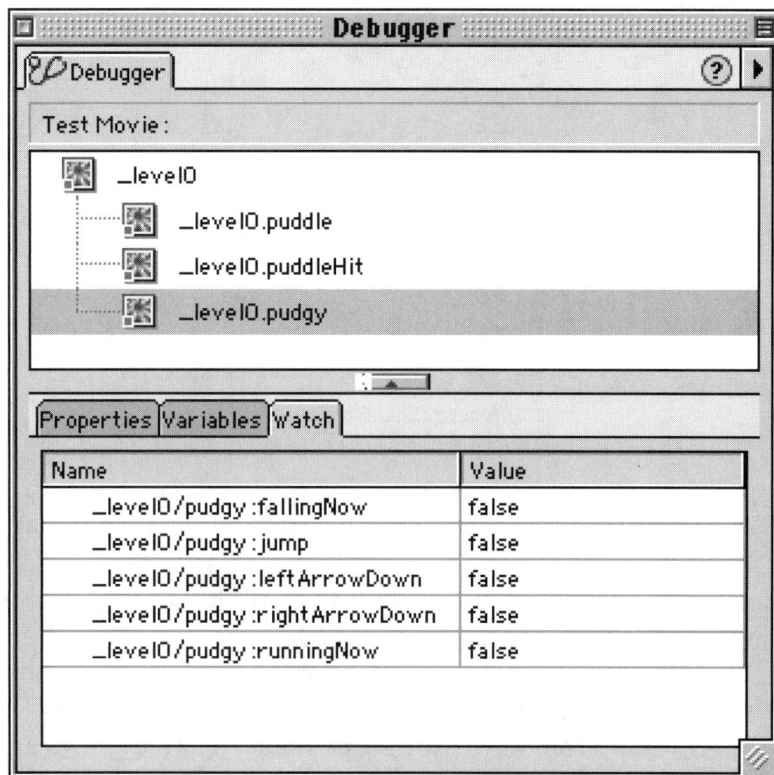

pudgy_done.fla

Changing Variables

1. Close the Debugger and the SWF file.
2. Open Scene 1.
3. Click on the frame in the actions layer and open the Frame Actions panel.
4. The code is:
   ```
   // Set global values for how high and how far
   // Pudgy will jump when he does jump.
   // These are the values we'll change
   // in the Debugger window.
   distance = 150;
   height = 100;
   ```
5. Close the Actions panel.
6. Control → Debug Movie.
7. Close the Debugger.
8. Open a new Debugger by control-clicking or right-clicking on the movie and choosing Debugger.
9. In the Display list, click on _level0.
10. Click the Variables tab.
11. Change the `height` value to 250.
12. Change the `distance` value to 150.
13. Click on the SWF movie.
14. Pudgy flies much higher and further now.
    Now let's try to change some of the variables for Pudgy.
15. Click on _level0.pudgy.
16. Click the Variables tab.
17. Change the values of any of the variables.
18. Click back on the movie and start playing. Note that the values of the variables go back to their original values. This is happening because those values are continually set by the movie. You did change their values, but the movie then changed them back.

Use Constants When Changing Variables

One final note: when you're changing the value of variables with the Debugger, you must constants like:

```
7                fringe
```

You can't use expressions like:

```
x * 7            toString(followNum)
```

Notes:

_____

_____

_____

_____

_____

_____

_____

_____

_____

_____

Lesson 6.2

Troubleshoot Easily Using Comments

Pudgy's Object Actions Without Comments

```
onClipEvent(load)
{
  SetVars();
  this.gotoAndStop("standing");
  function SetVars()
  {
        sqrootHeight = Math.sqrt(_root.height);
        widthFactor = (2 * sqrootHeight) /
          _root.distance;
        yInitial = this._y;
        xIntitial = this._x;
        xForJump = 0;
        xIncrement = 5;
  }
}
onClipEvent(keyDown)
{
  if(!fallingNow)
  {
        if(Key.getCode() == Key.RIGHT)
        {
                rightArrowDown = true;
                this._xscale = 40;
                if((!runningNow) && (!jump))
                {
                        this.gotoAndPlay("running");
                        runningNow = true;
                }
                leftArrowDown = false;
                setDirectionToNeutral = false;
                xHop = 1 * xIncrement;
        }
        else if(Key.getCode() == Key.LEFT)
```

```
        {
            leftArrowDown = true;
            this._xscale = -40;
            if((!runningNow) && (!jump))
            {
                    this.gotoAndPlay("running");
                    runningNow = true;
            }
            rightArrowDown = false;
            setDirectionToNeutral = false;
            xHop = (-1) * xIncrement;
        }
        else if((Key.getCode() == Key.UP) && (!jump))
        {
            jump = true;
            this.gotoAndPlay("flying");
            SetVars();
        }
    }
}
onClipEvent(keyUp)
{
  if(!fallingNow)
  {
        if(Key.getCode() == Key.RIGHT)
        {
            runningNow = false;
            if(this.jump)
            {
                    setDirectionToNeutral = true;
            }
            else
            {
                    this.gotoAndStop("standing");
                    rightArrowDown = false;
                    xHop = 0;
            }
        }
        else if(Key.getCode() == Key.LEFT)
        {
            runningNow = false;
```

```
            if(this.jump)
            {
                    setDirectionToNeutral = true;
            }
            else
            {
                    this.gotoAndStop("standing");
                    runningNow = false;
                    leftArrowDown = false;
                    xHop = 0;
            }
        }
    }
}
onClipEvent(enterFrame)
{
  if((this.jump) && (xForJump <= _root.distance)
    && (!fallingNow))
  {
        yFactorStep1 = (widthFactor * xForJump) -
          sqrootHeight;
        yFactorStep2 = Math.pow(yFactorStep1, 2);
        yFactorFinal = _root.height - yFactorStep2;
        this._y = yInitial - yFactorFinal;
        this._x = this._x + xHop;
        xForJump = xForJump + 5;
  }
  else if(this.hitTest(_root.puddleHit))
  {
        if(!fallingNow)
        {
                fallingNow = true;
                this._x = _root.puddle._x;
                this.gotoAndPlay("falling");
        }
  }
  else
  {
        jump = false;
        fallingNow = false;
        if(setDirectionToNeutral)
```

```
        {
                leftArrowDown = false;
                rightArrowDown = false;
                xHop = 0;
                setDirectionToNeutral = false;
        }
        else if(rightArrowDown || leftArrowDown)
        {
                this._x = this._x + xHop;
                runningNow = true;
        }
        else
        {
                this.gotoAndStop("standing");
                runningNow = false;
        }
    }
}
```

Pudgy's Object Actions with Comments

```
onClipEvent(load)
{
  // set variables for jumping
  // this calls the function a few lines down.
  SetVars();

  //set bird at right frame
  this.gotoAndStop("standing");

  function SetVars()
  {
        // set variables for jumping
        // these variables are based
        // on the x-y equation
        // y = h - (2*sqrt(h)x/d - sqrt(h))^2, where
        // h = height of the jump and
        // d = distance of the jump
        // This is a variation of the equation
        // for a parabola, y = x^2
        sqrootHeight = Math.sqrt(_root.height);
        widthFactor = (2 * sqrootHeight) /
          _root.distance;
        yInitial = this._y;
        xIntitial = this._x;
        xForJump = 0;
        xIncrement = 5;
  }
}

onClipEvent(keyDown)
{
  // we don't want the bird responding to
  // directional commands if it's falling down
  if(!fallingNow)
  {
        //determine which arrow key, if any,
        // is pressed down
        if(Key.getCode() == Key.RIGHT)
        {
```

```
        // set the correct variable and
        // make sure the bird's facing
        // the right direction
        rightArrowDown = true;
        this._xscale = 40;

        // determine whether bird should be
        // running or not
        if((!runningNow) && (!jump))
        {
                this.gotoAndPlay("running");
                runningNow = true;
        }

        leftArrowDown = false;
        setDirectionToNeutral = false;
        xHop = 1 * xIncrement;
}
else if(Key.getCode() == Key.LEFT)
{
        // set the correct variable and make sure
        // the bird's facing the left direction
        leftArrowDown = true;
        this._xscale = -40;

        //determine whether bird should be
        // running or not
        if((!runningNow) && (!jump))
        {
                this.gotoAndPlay("running");
                runningNow = true;
        }

        rightArrowDown = false;
        setDirectionToNeutral = false;
        xHop = (-1) * xIncrement;
}
else if((Key.getCode() == Key.UP) && (!jump))
{
        //set the stage and begin the jump process
        jump = true;
```

```
                this.gotoAndPlay("flying");
                SetVars();
        }
    }
}

onClipEvent(keyUp)
{
  // we don't want the bird to be able to jump
  // while it's falling.
  if(!fallingNow)
  {
        if(Key.getCode() == Key.RIGHT)
        {
                // This section makes sure that the bird
                // doesn't land and run in place
                runningNow = false;
                if(this.jump)
                {
                        setDirectionToNeutral = true;
                }
                else
                {
                        this.gotoAndStop("standing");
                        rightArrowDown = false;
                        xHop = 0;
                }
        }
        else if(Key.getCode() == Key.LEFT)
        {
                // This section makes sure that the bird
                // doesn't land and run in place
                runningNow = false;
                if(this.jump)
                {
                        setDirectionToNeutral = true;
                }
                else
                {
                        this.gotoAndStop("standing");
                        runningNow = false;
```

```
                    leftArrowDown = false;
                    xHop = 0;
            }
        }
    }
}

onClipEvent(enterFrame)
{
  if((this.jump) && (xForJump <= _root.distance)
    && (!fallingNow))
  {
        // set jumping height
        yFactorStep1 = (widthFactor * xForJump) -
          sqrootHeight;
        yFactorStep2 = Math.pow(yFactorStep1, 2);
        yFactorFinal = _root.height - yFactorStep2;

        //actually move the object
        this._y = yInitial - yFactorFinal;
        this._x = this._x + xHop;

        //prepare for the next loop
        xForJump = xForJump + 5;
  }
  else if(this.hitTest(_root.puddleHit))
  {
        //the bird is falling
        if(!fallingNow)
        {
              // move Pudgy to the center of the puddle,
              // so he's falling in the water
              // so 1) the splash will make sense and
              // 2) he doesn't fall in the middle of
              // some grass
              fallingNow = true;
              this._x = _root.puddle._x;
              this.gotoAndPlay("falling");
        }
  }
  else
```

```
    {
            //turn off jumping
            jump = false;

            //turn off falling
            fallingNow = false;

            //if user let go of a direction key
            //while in flight, reset it now
            if(setDirectionToNeutral)
            {
                    leftArrowDown = false;
                    rightArrowDown = false;
                    xHop = 0;

                    //this variable's job is done
                    setDirectionToNeutral = false;
            }
            else if(rightArrowDown || leftArrowDown)
            {
                    //allows the user to move Pudgy in
                    //different directions without jumping
                    this._x = this._x + xHop;
                    runningNow = true;
            }
            else
            {
                    //Pudgy is standing still
                    this.gotoAndStop("standing");
                    runningNow = false;
            }
    }
}
```

Lesson 6.3

Test Your Movie by Listing Objects and Variables

Listing Objects and Variables

1. Test the movie.
2. Choose Debug → List Objects.
3. In the Output window, you should see
   ```
   Level #0: Frame=1
   Shape:
   Movie Clip: Frame=1 Target="_level0.puddleHit"
   Shape:
   Movie Clip: Frame=1 Target="_level0.puddle"
   Label="still"
   Shape:
   Shape: Movie Clip: Frame=16 Target="_level0.pudgy"
   Label="standing"
   Shape:
   ```
   This lists all of the objects in the movie, along with their initial values.
4. Choose Debug → List Variables.
5. In the Output window you should see:
   ```
   Level #0:
   Variable _level0.$version = "MAC 5,0,30,0"
   Variable _level0.distance = 150
   Variable _level0.height = 100
   Movie Clip: Target="_level0.pudgy"
   Variable _level0.pudgy.SetVars = [function]
   Variable _level0.pudgy.sqrootHeight = 10
   Variable _level0.pudgy.widthFactor =
      0.133333333333333
   Variable _level0.pudgy.yInitial = 127.05
   Variable _level0.pudgy.xIntitial = 114.3
   Variable _level0.pudgy.xForJump = 0
   Variable _level0.pudgy.xIncrement = 5
   Variable _level0.pudgy.jump = false
   Variable _level0.pudgy.fallingNow = false
   Variable _level0.pudgy.runningNow = false
   ```

This lists all of the variables that initially exist in the movie.

Lecture 7

Complex Scripting

Objectives

- Add More Complex Actions Using More Complex Scripting

- Simulate Elasticity with ActionScript

- Simulate Inertia with ActionScript

Lesson 7.1

Add More Complex Actions Using More Complex Scripting

pudgy1.fla

Controls and Events

There are three controls in the Pudgy movie:

- Left Arrow
  - Moves the bird horizontally to the left
- Right Arrow
  - Moves the bird horizontally to the right
- Up Arrow
  - Causes the bird to jump

Here are the events:

- When the bird is jumping, it is in the flying stage.
- When the bird is not moving, it is standing.
- When the bird is moving, but not jumping, it is running.
- The bird always faces the direction it is moving in.
- The bird can change direction mid-air.
- When the bird overlaps the puddle, it is falling.
- When the bird finishes falling, it disappears and the puddle splashes.
- When the puddle finishes splashing, the bird reappears and the puddle resets to still.

Notes:

pudgy1.fla

Math Behind the Jump

I'll make it easy—the equation we want is this:

$$y = h - (2x/d * \sqrt{h} - \sqrt{h})^2$$

h = height of the jump
d = the distance of the jump.

Notes:

_____

_____

_____

_____

_____

_____

_____

_____

_____

_____

_____

_____

pudgy1.fla

Flying Pseudocode (Event)

```
onClipEvent(keyDown)
{
        if Key == up arrow
        {
                jump = true
                initialize values for jumping
                  (SetVars)
                set bird to "flying"
        }
}
```

pudgy1.fla

Flying Pseudocode (Flying)

```
onClipEvent(enterFrame)
{
        if jump is true and xForJump <= distance
        {
                set jumping height
                actually move the object
                prepare for next loop
        }
}
```

pudgy1.fla

Pseudocode for Moving Bird Back and Forth Using Arrow Keys

```
onClipEvent(keyDown)
{
        if Key == left
        {
                        leftArrow = true
                        rightArrow = false
                        face the bird left
                        if bird isn't jumping, set to running
                        runningNow = true
        }
        else if Key == right
        {
                        leftArrow = false
                        rightArrow = true
                        face the bird right
                        if bird isn't jumping, set to running
                        runningNow = true
        }
        else if Key == up arrow
        {
                        jump = true
                        initialize values for jumping
                          (SetVars)
                        set bird to "flying"
        }
}

onClipEvent(keyUp)
{
        if Key == left
        {
                        leftArrown = false
                        runningNow = false
                        set bird to standing
        }
        else if Key == right
        {
```

```
                            leftArrow = false
                            runningNow = false
                            set bird to standing
            }
}

onClipEvent(enterFrame)
{
            if jump is true and xForJump <= distance
            {
                            set jumping height
                            actually move the object
                            prepare for next loop
            }
            else
            {
                            jump = false

                            if leftArrowDown or rightArrowDown
                            {
                                            move bird
                                            runningNow = true
                            }
                            else
                            {
                                            make bird stand
                                            runningNow = false
                            }
            }
}
```

pudgy1.fla

Code for Every Frame

- The majority of real action takes place inside the `enterFrame` section.
- The other events set the variables that the `enterFrame` section uses to make decisions about which action to take.
- The only real actions that occur outside of `enterFrame` are those that move the playhead of the Pudgy movie clip.

Notes:

_____

_____

_____

_____

_____

_____

_____

_____

_____

_____

pudgy1.fla

Pseudocode for Falling Into Puddle

```
onClipEvent(keyDown)
{
        if the bird is NOT falling
        {
                if Key == left
                {
                        leftArrown = true
                        rightArrow = false
                        face the bird left
                        if bird isn't jumping,
                          set to running
                        runningNow = true
                }
                else if Key == right
                {
                        leftArrown = false
                        rightArrow = true
                        face the bird right
                        if bird isn't jumping,
                          set to running
                        runningNow = true
                }
                else if Key == up arrow
                {
                        jump = true
                        initialize values for
                          jumping (SetVars)
                        set bird to "flying"
                }
        }
}

onClipEvent(keyUp)
{
        if the bird is NOT falling
        {
                if Key == left
                {
```

```
                                        leftArrown = false
                                        runningNow = false
                                        set bird to standing
                          }
                          else if Key == right
                          {
                                        leftArrown = false
                                        runningNow = false
                                        set bird to standing
                          }
                }
        }


onClipEvent(enterFrame)
{
        if jump is true and xForJump <= distance
        {
                        set jumping height
                        actually move the object
                        prepare for next loop
        }
        else if bird is over puddle
        {
                        fallingNow = true
                        set bird playhead to "falling"
        }
        else
        {
                        jump = false

                        if leftArrowDown or rightArrowDown
                        {
                                        move bird
                                        runningNow = true
                        }
                        else
                        {
                                        make bird stand
                                        runningNow = false
                        }
                }
        }
}
```

pudgy1.fla

Frame Action for Last Frame of "`falling`"

```
stop();
_root.puddle.gotoAndPlay("splashing");
```

Frame Action for First Frame of "`splashing`"

```
// Move Pudgy outside the puddle and hide him
// so the falling isn't triggered again
_root.pudgy._visible = false;
_root.pudgy._x = 50;
```

Frame Action for Last Frame in the "`splashing`" Section

```
// Reset Pudgy's stats and position
_root.pudgy._visible = true;
_root.pudgy._xscale = 40;
_root.pudgy.fallingNow = false;
_root.pudgy.rightArrowDown = false;
_root.pudgy.leftArrowDown = false;

// set Pudgy to be standing still
_root.pudgy.gotoAndPlay("standing");

// move the puddle's playhead to calmness once again
gotoAndStop("still");
```

pudgy1.fla

Tweaking the Jump

```
onClipEvent(keyUp)
{
        if the bird is NOT falling
        {
                if Key == left
                {
                        if bird is jumping
                        {
setDirectionToNeutral = true
                        }
                        else
                        {
                                leftArrown
                                  = false
                                runningNow
                                  = false
                                set bird to
                                  standing
                        }
                }
                else if Key == right
                {
                        if bird is jumping
                        {
setDirectionToNeutral = true
                        }
                        else
                        {
                                leftArrown
                                  = false
                                runningNow
                                  = false
                                set bird to
                                  standing
                        }
                }
        }
}
```

```
onClipEvent(enterFrame)
{
        if jump is true and xForJump <= distance
        {
                set jumping height
                actually move the object
                prepare for next loop
        }
        else if bird is over puddle
        {
                fallingNow = true
                set bird playhead to "falling"
        }
        else
        {
                jump = false
                if setDirectionToNeutral
                {
                        leftArrowDown = false
                        rightArrowDown = false
                        setDirectionToNeutral =
                            false
                }
                else if leftArrowDown or rightArrow
                  Down
                {
                        move bird
                        runningNow = true
                }
                else
                {
                    make bird stand
                    runningNow = false
                }
        }
}
```

pudgy1.fla

All the Code (found in List7-1.txt)

```
onClipEvent(load)
{
        // set variables for jumping
        // this calls the function a few lines down.
        SetVars();

        //set bird at right frame
        this.gotoAndStop("standing");

        function SetVars()
        {
                // set variables for jumping
                // these variables are
                // based on the x-y equation
                // y = h - (2*sqrt(h)x/d -
                  sqrt(h))^2, where
                // h = height of the jump and
                // d = distance of the jump
                // This is a variation of the
                  equation
                // for a parabola, y = x^2
                sqrootHeight = Math.sqrt
                  (_root.height);
                widthFactor = (2 * sqrootHeight) /
                  _root.distance;
                yInitial = this._y;
                xInitial = this._x;
                xForJump = 0;
                xIncrement = 5;
        }
}

onClipEvent(keyDown)
{
        // we don't want the bird responding
        // to directional commands if it's falling down
        if(!fallingNow)
        {
```

```
                              // determine which arrow key, if any,
                              // is pressed down
                              if(Key.getCode() == Key.RIGHT)
                              {
                                              // set the correct
                                                variable and make sure
                                              // the bird's facing the
                                                right direction
                                              rightArrowDown = true;
                                              this._xscale = 40;

                                              // determine whether
                                                bird
                                              // should be running or
                                                not
                                              if((!runningNow) &&
                                                (!jump))
                                              {
this.gotoAndPlay("running");
                                                              runningNow
                                                                = true;
                                              }

                                              leftArrowDown = false;
                                              setDirectionToNeutral =
                                                false;
                                              xHop = 1 * xIncrement;
                              }
                              else if(Key.getCode() == Key.LEFT)
                              {
                                              // set the correct
                                                variable and make sure
                                              // the bird's facing the
                                                left direction
                                              leftArrowDown = true;
                                              this._xscale = -40;

                                              // determine whether
                                                bird
```

```
                                        // should be running or
                                           not
                                        if((!runningNow) &&
                                           (!jump))
                                        {
this.gotoAndPlay("running");

                                                    runningNow
                                                    = true;
                                        }

                                        rightArrowDown = false;
                                        setDirectionToNeutral =
                                           false;
                                        xHop = (-1) * xIncre
                                           ment;
                            }
                            else if((Key.getCode() == Key.UP) &&
                               (!jump))
                            {
                                        // set the stage and
                                           begin the jump process
                                        jump = true;
                                        this.gotoAndPlay
                                           ("flying");
                                        SetVars();

                            }
                }
        }


onClipEvent(keyUp)
{
        // we don't want the bird to be able to jump
        // while it's falling.
        if (!fallingNow)
        {
                    if(Key.getCode() == Key.RIGHT)
                    {
                                // This section makes
                                   sure that the bird
                                // doesn't land and run
                                   in place
```

```
                                        runningNow = false;
                                        if(this.jump)
                                        {

setDirectionToNeutral = true;
                                        }
                                        else
                                        {

this.gotoAndStop("standing");
                                                    rightArrowDown =
                                                      false;
                                                    xHop = 0;
                                        }
                        }
                        else if(Key.getCode() == Key.LEFT)
                        {
                                        // This section makes
                                          sure that the bird
                                        // doesn't land and run
                                          in place
                                        runningNow = false;
                                        if (this.jump)
                                        {

setDirectionToNeutral = true;
                                        }
                                        else
                                        {

this.gotoAndStop("standing");
                                                    runningNow =
                                                      false;
                                                    leftArrowDown =
                                                      false;
                                                    xHop = 0;
                                        }
                        }
            }
}


onClipEvent(enterFrame)
{
        if((this.jump) &&
```

```
            (xForJump <= _root.distance) &&
            (!fallingNow))
  {
            // set jumping height
            yFactorStep1 = (widthFactor * xFor
               Jump) - sqrootHeight;
            yFactorStep2 = Math.pow(yFactorStep1,
               2);
            yFactorFinal = _root.height -
               yFactorStep2;

            // actually move the object
            this._y = yInitial - yFactorFinal;
            this._x = this._x + xHop;

            // prepare for next loop
            xForJump = xForJump + 5;
  }
  else if(this.hitTest(_root.puddleHit))
  {
            // the bird is falling
            if(!fallingNow)
            {
                        // move Pudgy to the
                           center of the puddle,
                        // so he's falling in
                           the water
                        // so 1) the splash will
                           make sense and
                        // 2) he doesn't fall in
                           the middle of
                        // some grass
                        fallingNow = true;
                        this._x = _root.
                           puddle._x;
                        this.gotoAndPlay
                           ("falling");
            }

  }
  else
  {
```

```
                    // turn off jumping
                    jump = false;

                    //turn off falling
                    fallingNow = false;

                    // if user let go of a direction key
                    // while in flight, reset it now
                    if(setDirectionToNeutral)
                    {
                              leftArrowDown = false;
                              rightArrowDown = false;
                              xHop = 0;

                              // this variable's job
                                 is done
                              setDirectionToNeutral =
                                 false;
                    }
                    else if(rightArrowDown || left
                      ArrowDown)
                    {
                              // allows the user to
                                 move Pudgy in
                              // different directions
                                 without jumping
                              this._x = this._x +
                                 xHop;
                              runningNow = true;
                    }
                    else
                    {
                              // Pudgy is standing
                                 still
                              this.gotoAndStop
                                 ("standing");
                              runningNow = false;
                    }
               }
          }
```

Lesson 7.2

Simulate Elasticity with ActionScript

Cool Stuff

```
http://www.praystation.com
```

elasticity.fla

Action-Only Movie Clips

Frame 1 Series of Actions
Frame 2 `gotoAndPlay(1)`

The first frame has a series of actions, and the second frame has only one action: `gotoAndPlay(1)`. That way, we have a constantly recurring set of actions. This method can take a little getting used to, but it's a great way to create modular, easily reused code.

Notes:

_____

_____

_____

_____

_____

_____

_____

_____

_____

_____

elasticity.fla

Auto-Build Movie Clip

```
if(_root.currentClip < 6)
{
        duplicateMovieClip("_root." + _root.currentClip,
          _root.currentClip+1, _root.currentClip+1);
        _root.currentClip = _root.currentClip+1;
}
else
{
        stop();
}
```

This code creates the six boxes, based on duplicating the first one. The initial value of currentClip is set by the main movie's frame actions:

```
// set variables
currentClip = 1;
```

elasticity.fla

What the Chain Movie Clip Does

The chain movie clip does several things:

- Creates a duplicate of the line movie clip.
- Positions the duplicated line onto the appropriate box.
- Angles the duplicated line clip.
- Moves the box according to the elasticity rules.

Notes:

_____

_____

_____

_____

_____

_____

_____

_____

_____

_____

elasticity.fla

The Chain Movie Clip

```
// This is the code that really creates the elasticity

// The line in question is duplicated,
// moved to the position of the box,
// and stretched appropriately.
// Then, the box is moved according to
// some math that determines the elasticity

// The previous clip is the one above the current clip.
// That is, if this is box #2, its
// name is "2" and the one above it is "1"
// Predictably, the top box - the one the user can drag,
// is named "0"
// Since each "chain" clip is inside a box clip,
// we have to look at the box clip's
// name, and then take one from that to get
// the name of the next box

boxNumber = _parent._name;
thisLineName = "_root.line" + boxNumber;

boxX = _parent._x;
boxY = _parent._y

previousBox = "_root." + (boxNumber - 1);

previousBoxX = getProperty(previousBox, _x)
previousBoxY = getProperty(previousBox, _y)


// Now, we'll modify the line that connects
// this box to the previous one
// this line creates a new movie clip and
// places it on a high level
duplicateMovieClip("_root.line", "line" + boxNumber,
boxNumber + 100);
```

```
// Now we'll set the properties of the line:
// its x and y position, and
// its xscale and yscale
// We have to use setProperty, because
// we're dynamically figuring out which clip this is,
// and we have to use boxName to figure that out.

// First, we set the x and y coordinates
// to be the same as the box's
setProperty(thisLineName, _x, _parent._x);
setProperty(thisLineName, _y, _parent._y);
// Now, we set the xscale and yscale of this line,
// so that it's the right shape
// and facing in the right direction
setProperty(thisLineName, _xscale, previousBoxX - boxX);
setProperty(thisLineName, _yscale, previousBoxY - boxY);

// Move the box
// The numbers here determine the
// elastic properties of the movie
// Increase the divisor to slow down the elasticity
// Decrease the divisor to speed up the elasticity
// The best way to understand what's going on here
// is to play with the numbers
setProperty(_parent, _x, (boxX + (previousBoxX - boxX)/
  2) + 2);
setProperty(_parent, _y, (boxY + (previousBoxY - boxY)/
  2) + 12);
```

Lesson 7.3

Simulate Inertia with ActionScript

inertia.fla

coast

The `coast` code does the following:

- Determines the new position of the box, based on the horizontal and vertical speed at which it was moving.
- Adjusts the box's speed, based on the inertia rules.
- Sees if the box has traveled beyond the boundaries; if so, makes it appear at the opposite side.

Notes:

_____

_____

_____

_____

_____

_____

_____

_____

inertia.fla

The Box Clip

There are several parts to the box clip:

- The box frame and the crosshairs (the `"content"` layer);
- A transparent button;
- The inertia movie clip;
- Some frame actions.

Notes:

_____

_____

_____

_____

_____

_____

_____

_____

_____

_____

_____

inertia.fla

Box's Frame Actions

```
// set variables for dragging and inertia

// edges of box
left = 3;
top = 3;
bottom = 220;
right = 425;

sizeOfTarget = 22;
minX = left - sizeOfTarget;
maxX = right + sizeOfTarget;
minY = top - sizeOfTarget;
maxY = bottom + sizeOfTarget;

// Set factor of decreasing speed
// if this is greater than 1, the box
// will endlessly accelerate.
friction = 0.96;
```

inertia.fla

Button Over Box

```
on(press)
{
        startDrag(this, false, left, top, right, bottom);

        // start setting the horizontal speed and
        // vertical speed as determined by the user
        // dragging the box.
        inertia.gotoAndPlay("map");
}


on(release, releaseOutside)
{
        stopDrag();

        // initiate the coasting to a stop
        inertia.gotoAndPlay("coast");
}
```

Inertia Movie Clip

Map

```
// get current coordinates of the box
newX = _parent._x;
newY = _parent._y;

// set horizontal and vertical speed
_parent.xspeed = (newX - oldX)*0.5;
_parent.yspeed = (newY - oldY)*0.5;

// prepare for next movement
oldX = newX;
oldY = newY;
```

Inertia Movie Clip

Coast

First, some pseudocode:

```
Move the box to the new position, based on current speed.
Change speed based on how much friction exists
If the box has moved too far right, move it to the left
edge.
If the box has moved too far left, move it to the right
edge.
If the box has moved too far down, move it to the top
edge.
If the box has moved too far up, move it to the bottom
edge.
```

That's it! Here's the actual code:

```
// set new position of square
_parent._x = _parent._x + _parent.xspeed;
_parent._y = _parent._y + _parent.yspeed;

// adjust speed according to friction rules
_parent.xspeed = _parent.xspeed * _parent.friction;
_parent.yspeed = _parent.yspeed * _parent.friction;

// wrap-around effect
if(_parent._x > _parent.maxX)
{
        _parent._x = _parent.minX;
}
else if(_parent._x < _parent.minX)
{
        _parent._x = _parent.maxX;
}
else if(_parent._y > _parent.maxY)
{
        _parent._y = _parent.minY;
}
else if(_parent._y < _parent.minY)
{
        _parent._y = _parent.maxY;
}
```

Lecture 8

Further Applications for Flash

Objectives:

- Create a Simple Preloader Movie

- Create a Minimizing Window Pane

- Create a Scrolling Text Box with a Slider

Lesson 8.1

Create a Simple Preloader Movie

preloader.fla

Create a Simple Preloader Movie

- Open preloader.fla.
- There are three layers:
  - actions
  - preloader
  - baubles
- The preloader is a simple movie clip that covers the baubles until the baubles have finished loading. Then the preloader disappears.
- Look at the actions layer, and its single line of actionscript:
    ```
    preloader._visible = false.
    ```
- The actions on this frame layer aren't run until the movie has completed loaded.
- Make sure that when you publish your movie, your load order is "top down." This ensures that the preloader will appear before the baubles do. Look under File → Publish Settings.

Notes:

_____

_____

_____

_____

_____

Lesson 8.2

Create a Minimizing Window Pane

windowshade_1.fla

Create a Minimizing Window Pane

1. Open up windowshade_1.fla.
2. Open the Library. Notice there are three symbols: two movie clips and a transparent button.

The "main pane" symbol is the large window. The title bar, along with the "main pane" is in the "window pane" movie clip. Note the name of the window pane is "window1" on the Stage.

Inside the window pane movie, there are three transparent buttons: one long one and two small ones.

Notes:

_____

_____

_____

_____

_____

_____

_____

windowshade1.fla

Dragging the Window

1. Open the window pane symbol.
2. Click on the long button.
3. Enter this code:

```
on(press)
{
   startDrag(_root.window1, false);
}

on(release)
{
   stopDrag();
}
```

4. Test the movie.

Nothing too wildly interesting here. You've seen `startDrag` before. Let's add the action for the "kill this window" button (the one on the far right).

1. Click on the right button.
2. Enter this code:

```
on(press)
{
   _root.window1._visible = false;
}
```

3. Test the movie. Poof! The window disappears.

Again, not exactly a magic show. Now let's check out the interesting action.

1. Click on the left small button.
2. Enter this code:

```
on(press)
{
  if(_root.window1.mainpane._visible)
  {
        _root.window1.mainpane._visible = false;
  }
  else
  {
        _root.window1.mainpane._visible = true;
  }
}
```

We're using a little trick and getting around have to use variables. notice that we're seeing if the main pane is visible or not, and then doing the opposite. If the window is visible, we make it invisible. If it's invisible, we make it visible.

3. Test the movie. The left button turns the main pane on and off.

Lesson 8.3

Create a Scrolling Text Box with a Slider

scroll_1.fla

Parts of the Text Box

Our little text box system will eventually consist of the following parts:

- a text window
- a string of text
- two arrow buttons
- a slider button
- 3 actionscript-only movie clips. These three clips will handle the text's scrolling for the up button, the down button, and the slider—each method of scrolling gets its own actionscript-only movie clip.

Notes:

_____

_____

_____

_____

_____

_____

_____

scroll_1.fla

Text Window and a String of Text

1. Open up `scroll_1.fla` from your hard drive.
2. Notice that Scene 1 is composed of a single movie clip called "`window`".
3. Open the Library.
4. Double-click the "`window`" movie clip symbol.
5. Click on the text box. Notice that it's a dynamic text box, and we've called it "`scrolltext`."
6. Notice the two arrows. Notice the little slider box (it's gray). Click on it. This movie is called "`scroll drag mc`" in the Library and "`slider`" on the Stage.
7. Open up the "`window`" symbol.
8. Click on the frame in the "`actions`" layer.
9. Open the Actions panel (make sure it's on Frame Actions)
10. Enter the following code (definitely copy and paste from the file `scrolltext.txt`, which you copied to your hard drive from the CD):

```
scrolltext = "Lorem ipsum dolor sit amet, con-
sectetuer adipiscing elit, sed diam nonummy nibh eu-
ismod tincidunt ut laoreet dolore magna aliquam erat
volutpat. Ut wisi enim ad minim veniam, quis nostrud
exercitation ulliam corper suscipit lobortis nisl ut
aliquip ex ea commodo consequat. Duis autem veleum
iriure dolor in hendrerit in vulputate velit esse mo-
lestie consequat, vel willum lunombro dolore eu feu-
giat nulla facilisis at vero eros et accumsan et
iusto odio dignissim qui blandit praesent luptatum
zzril delenit augue duis dolore te feugait nulla fa-
cilisi. Li Europan lingues es membres del sam fami-
lie. Lor separat existentie es un myth. Por scientie,
musica, sport etc., li tot Europa usa li sam vocabu-
larium. Li lingues differe solmen in li grammatica,
li pronunciation e li plu commun vocabules. Omnicos
directe al desirabilit de un nov lingua franca: on
refusa continuar payar custosi traductores. It solmen
va esser necessi far uniform grammatica, pronuncia-
tion e plu sommun paroles. Ma quande lingues coa-
```

```
lesce, li grammatica del resultant lingue es plu sim-
plic e regulari quam ti del coalescent lingues. Li
nov lingua franca va esser plu simplic e regulari
quam li existent Europan lingues. It va esser tam
simplic quam Occidental: in fact, it va esser Occi-
dental. A un Angleso it va semblar un simplificat An-
gles, quam un skeptic Cambridge amico dit me que
Occidental es.";

stop();
```

11. Test the movie! The text box should now fill with the text.

scroll_1.fla

scrollDown

1. Choose Insert → New Symbol.
2. Call it *scrollDown* and make sure it's a movie clip.
3. Give this movie clip three keyframes.
4. In the first frame, enter this code:

```
stop();
```

5. In the second frame, enter this code:

```
currentScroll = _parent.scrolltext.scroll;
max = _parent.scrolltext.maxscroll;

if (currentScroll < max)
{
  // move the text
  _parent.scrolltext.scroll = currentScroll + 1;
}
```

6. And in the final frame, enter:

```
gotoAndPlay(2);
```

7. Go back to the "window" movie clip and drag the "scrollDown" movie clip somewhere near the down arrow. It will appear in the movie as a little dot. Be sure to call it "*scrollDown*" in the Instance panel.
8. Go to the window movie clip.
9. Click on the down arrow.
10. Open the actions panel.
11. Enter this code:

```
on (press)
{
  scrolldown.gotoAndPlay(2);
}
```

```
on (release)
{
  scrolldown.gotoAndStop(1);
}
```

12. Test the movie! You can now scroll down.

scroll_1.fla

Scrolling Up

1. Create a duplicate of the `scrollDown` movie clip.
2. Rename the copy *"scrollUp"*.
3. Open up `scrollUp`.
4. Go to frame 2.
5. Replace the code in frame 2 with this:

```
currentScroll = _parent.scrolltext.scroll-1;

if (currentScroll > 0)
{
   // move the text
   _parent.scrolltext.scroll = currentScroll -1;
}
```

6. Drag "`scrollUp`" into the window movie clip and call it "`scrollUp`" in the Instance panel.
7. Go to the window movie clip.
8. Click on the up arrow.
9. Enter this code:

```
on (press)
{
   scrollup.gotoAndPlay(2);
}

on (release)
{
   scrollup.gotoAndStop(1);
}
```

10. Test the movie!

scroll_1.fla

Positioning the Slider

1. Go to Scene 1.
2. Click on the frame in the Actions layer.
3. Enter this code:

```
sliderRange = 130;
sliderYStart = -64;

window.slider._y = sliderYStart;

stop();
```

4. Open the `scrollDown` movie clip.
5. Click on the second frame.
6. Add this code:

```
if (currentScroll <= max)
{
  //move the little scroll thingie
  scrollPercentage = currentScroll/max;
  sliderOffset = scrollPercentage*_root.sliderRange;
  _root.window.slider._y = _root.sliderYStart + slid-
erOffset;
}
```

7. Test the movie!

Now let's do the same with the `scrollUp`.

1. Open the `scrollUp` movie clip.
2. Go to the second frame.
3. Add this code:

```
max = _parent.scrolltext.maxscroll;

if (currentScroll >= 0)
{
  //move the slider
  scrollPercentage = currentScroll/max;
```

```
    sliderOffset = scrollPercentage*_root.sliderRange;

    _root.window.slider._y = _root.sliderYStart +
       sliderOffset;
}
```

4. Test the movie! That slider's moving around all over the place.

scroll_1.fla

Dragging the Slider

1. Make a duplicate of either `scrollUp` or `scrollDown` and call it `scrollGeneral`.
2. Go to frame 2.
3. Replace the code with this:

```
//set scrolling
currentY = _root.window.slider._y;
Ypercentage = (currentY -
_root.sliderYStart)/(_root.sliderRange);

max = _root.window.scrolltext.maxscroll;

scrollValue = Math.round(Ypercentage*max);

if (scrollValue < 1)
{
scrollValue = 1;
}

_root.window.scrolltext.scroll = scrollValue;
```

4. Go to "`Scroll drag mc`" and click on the button.
5. Enter this code as an Object Action:

```
on(press)
{

startDrag(this,false,160,_root.sliderYStart,160,_root
  .sliderRange+_root.sliderYStart);
  _root.window.scrollGeneral.gotoAndPlay(2);
}

on(release)
{
  stopDrag();
  _root.window.scrollGeneral.gotoAndStop(1);
}
```

6. Test the movie! Yahoo! It works!

Contact Your Instructor

E-mail me at :

```
flash@wire-man.com
```

with any questions you have and feel free to check out my site at:

```
http://www.wire-man.com/flash5.
```